$mall business

george w. rimler/neil j. humphreys

developing the winning management team

People are the most important resource in any organization. But in a small business, where there is little room for error and few resources to fall back on when mistakes are made, choosing the right staff is absolutely essential. This book is intended to show the small business manager how effective personnel management can substantially increase the likelihood of success for his or her company.

One of the major reasons for the high failure rate of small businesses is poor management. Although many books have been published to help the small business manager increase effectiveness in technical areas such as accounting, budgeting, and marketing, this is the first book to concentrate on developing the human resources within an organization. George Rimler and Neil Humphreys discuss the importance of hiring the right people, providing meaningful training in all phases of development, and developing employees for first-line, middle, and top management positions to ensure the availability of qualified individuals who will support growth in the firm. In addition, the authors stress the importance of understanding succession as it relates to business growth, development, and the continuity of an organization beyond the tenure or life of its original owner.

It is not difficult to start a small business; the difficulty lies in keeping it going, and seeing that it grows, develops, and prospers. So if you own or are thinking of starting or purchasing a small business, this book will be an essential tool in helping ensure its success.

Small
developing the winning

a division of

business
management team

**george w. rimler
neil j. humphreys**

american management associations

Library of Congress Cataloging in Publication Data

Rimler, George W.
  Small business.

  Includes index.
  1. Small business—Personnel management. I. Humphreys, Neil J., 1934–
joint author. II. Title.
HF5549.R535   658.3'03   79-54848
ISBN 0-8144-5581-6

© 1980 AMACOM
A division of American Management Associations, New York.

First Printing

to our parents

preface

SMALL BUSINESS is the dominant form of business enterprise in the United States. From photocopying to steel manufacturing, small firms have often led the large ones in innovation. According to recent Small Business Administration (SBA) figures, there are over 8 million small business firms in the United States accounting for 43 percent of the Gross National Product. In addition, small business has served as a vehicle for upward mobility in many societies. For European and Latin American immigrants in the United States or for Asian immigrants in England, the ability to start and sustain small firms has been essential for economic advancement.

Just what is a small firm? In an attempt to find a definition of this term, many different standards have been used: number of employees, dollar assets, sales volume, number of locations, and so on. But no quantitative criterion can really define the small firm. A small firm is one in which ownership and management are vitally intertwined, one in which there is an active involvement of ownership in management. The small firm responds to the owner's values and views; indeed, the small firm may best be viewed as an owner-managed firm. Many books have attempted to improve the chances of a small business's success by helping the manager improve his or her technical ability in accounting, production, or marketing. This book, however, aims to improve the small business manager's ability to develop the *human* assets within the enterprise.

A manager must work through others. Often the small business manager begins an enterprise on the basis of technical ability, but the small business manager's ability to deal effectively and positively with the people inside and outside the company is the key to determining the firm's success or failure. A successful small firm must develop its people to their full potential, and it is to this end that we dedicate this book.

George W. Rimler
Neil J. Humphreys

contents

1

To be what we are and to become what we are capable of becoming, is the only end in life.

ROBERT LOUIS STEVENSON

have you thought about owning a business?

"Tourist attraction—established, unique tour service in historic western state capital city with excellent expansion opportunities." "Manufacturing plant—L.A. area, aircraft parts, North Carolina equipment, will consider trade." "For sale—established, upstate N.Y. fast-food restaurant and lounge. Excellent location on major highway." "Outstanding retail location—shoes and leather accessories. Completely furnished. Owner wishes to sell." "Successful executive, experience in sales and manufacture of small electric consumer appliances, seeks partnership or sole ownership of established business." Each of these brief advertisements have two things in common: they are offering some kind of small business opportunity for sale, and they are typical of those seen every day in newspapers and journals throughout the country.

Why would people want to buy a business with all of its potential problems when they can probably get a job and work for someone else? The pay in working for someone else is good and there are fewer headaches. Many people who read these classified business advertisements would probably not have much interest in answering them. A small segment of the population, however, would read these ads with a great deal of enthusiasm, and this book is written for them—people who are, or might be, interested in owning their own small businesses.

Is the person who is interested in owning a business rather than working for someone else much different from other people? Probably not. And what great skills does this person possess that the majority lacks? Probably none! But people willing to risk business ownership probably differ somewhat in their make-up: they feel some things more strongly than the majority of people.

What Drives the Small Business Owner?

Potential business owners are people who have developed a strong desire to "do their own thing" rather than be directed by others. People in this category are interested in new things, are willing to explore different possibilities, and aren't afraid to risk both time and money in an effort to satisfy their material and psychological needs. Traditionally, this kind of person was called an entrepreneur. The word entrepreneur is defined in the dictionary as "the person who organizes, manages, and assumes the risks of a business; a successful businessman." It is taken from the French word *entreprendre*—to undertake.

The characteristics shown on page 3 are typical of the contrasting profile between entrepreneurs and those who work for other people.

The common thread in each characteristic is doing things for yourself when you're the entrepreneur as opposed to letting things be done for you when you work for someone else.

	Works for Oneself	*Works for Others*
Achievement	Depends on one's own ability	Part of "system" that may be more important than individual ability.
Risk	Reputation, capital	Relatively small when one conforms to the system. Dismissal in extreme cases.
Attention to detail	Ultimate responsibility	Controlled, to some extent, by those above in the hierarchy.
Commitment	Total, always on call	Limited (9:00 A.M.–5:00 P.M.)
Time management	Left to one's own devices	Controlled by company policy to large extent.
Control	Wants to control one's own activities.	Willing to allow control by others.
Venture	Looks for fresh ideas and new ways of doing things.	Often depends on tradition; not usually willing to experiment.

What Happens When You Work for Someone Else?

The person described in the right column is in a sense controlled by "organizational insulation." In many instances, individual actions are protected by the umbrella of company policy and organizational tradition. This attracts certain kinds of people, because such policy softens or eliminates the bumps resulting from poor decisions. The person can make decisions with less risk about their consequences, because protection is provided through the system. As with any insulation, there is a restriction of some element, and organizational insulation is no exception to the rule. The same system that protects individual employees from potential errors in judgment also prohibits the free flow of their ideas.

Of course, every company has some form of suggestion system in which employees are encouraged to submit ideas for improving the work situation in their areas. But suggestions that may be harmful to the system are invariably rejected by some individual or by a committee, and even successful suggestions are usually thoroughly "laundered" before they are approved for use. Consequently, it is unusual for significant harm to come to the organization as a result of a new idea generated by an individual in the ranks.

The Small Business Owner Operates Alone

Small business operators have little or no protection of this kind. The success of day-to-day company operations depends on their decisions, because there is no insulation protecting them from the outside world. Good decisions mean that their business has a chance for continued growth and success. Poor decisions, however, ensure the business's failure—the only unknown quantity is when it will happen.

People have fears: some people fear height, while others fear closed-in places. Everyone fears failure, particularly where their jobs are concerned. When fear of failure regarding a job is high, people search for some means to lessen their chances of failure. The trade-off for protection is often individual conformity, and those who are afraid are willing to pay the price and to abide by the company rules and policies. No one speaks of organizational insulation in large companies; the correct term is security, but it means the same thing.

Does this mean that small business people are not afraid? No, but their fear of individual failure is not strong enough to overcome their faith in their own ability. They don't need the protection of a big company. These people are willing to stand on their own decisions, their own abilities, and their own knowledge of what they can accomplish. They are not willing to exchange their own potential for the security that is supposedly found in large companies. Fear and security thus become the basic rationale for determining differences in the job profile of the entrepreneur and of the employee. People often work for others, rather than for themselves, where a greater degree of security is necessary for them to overcome their fear of job failure.

The Opportunity for Innovation Is Real in Small Business

Entrepreneurs are associated with new ideas and new concepts which they develop and then market. Two examples of this were the Polaroid Land Camera and the Xeroxographic process. Both ideas were new, and each one was introduced by a single entrepreneur. Today, the instant camera and the photocopy process both hold important positions in the industrial arena. But not everyone can invent a new technological process, providing them with a made-to-order business. Most small business owners are managers of someone else's ideas. The man who owns a McDonald's franchise is a manager. The woman controlling three franchise 7-Eleven stores is a manager.

The small business person who starts a traditional type of business usually duplicates what already exists. The skills needed to start a business may be quite different from those necessary to maintain it. Entrepreneurial skills are usually needed to start a business, but managerial skills are necessary to maintain the business and make it really grow. Today, a majority of owners—but only a minority of entrepreneurs—is involved in small business operations. A manager can be successful in small business today without having to produce a totally original product line or service.

Success: Potential Problem for Small Business

Some of the characteristics that are essential for people who go into business may not help them in managing other people. Quite possibly, the imaginative qualities in the individual may become the seeds of self-destruction as the business develops and grows. Initially, the responsibility for the operation falls on the owner-manager, and its success depends entirely on his or her personality and areas of expertise. But business success demands a new pattern, one that shifts the focus away from the owner in many ways. It becomes necessary for the owner to conduct an orchestra and discard the initial "one-man band" role. This is a most traumatic change, and one that is close to impossible for some small business entrepreneurs to accept.

Instead of the self-centered dependence characterized in formative growth years, the larger business operation demands an "other-centered" operation whose focus is the newly acquired employees. This transition may conjure up memories of the very situation that caused the owner to leave another job and open a business (although this time the owner is on the opposite side of the table from the employees).

Consider the owner who opened her own business because she felt that her former job would not allow her to contribute all that she could. It was hard to gain someone's ear to make suggestions, and she was often told to do her job and not worry about things outside her domain. She obviously felt underutilized, so she quit. Now she gets very upset with her employees if they seem to be goofing off rather than working hard on their jobs. She cannot, or will not, recognize her *own* characteristics and individual motivation in other people when they are trying to stretch *their* roles and make a more significant contribution. Is this inconsistent behavior? Possibly, but the primary relationship has changed from that of employee to that of owner and employer, and that is a significant change.

Growth affects the individual owner when it leads to orderliness. This may seem to be a contradiction, but innovation and orderliness cannot occur simultaneously for some entrepreneurs whose concept of innovation hinges on their being able to do things as they want to when they want to in every sense. This may be proper behavior for the individual who is just starting out, but success and its concomitant growth demand more order and routine. At this point, what had been fun for the owner may become a bore. Something has changed. The inconsistency grows in the mind of the entrepreneur. The entrepreneur's freewheeling, innovative way of life is over, and he has become a prisoner of what had once been his toy. His interest wanes, and soon he prepares to begin yet another search for the Holy Grail. No wonder some people who have vast material wealth cannot find the peace and happiness they seek!

Management Universally Requires New Skills

Business innovators suffer from the same malady found in other walks of life. A good athlete will not necessarily be a good coach. An excellent classroom teacher can become a horrible department administrator. Many a top salesman has seen his career deteriorate after he was promoted to sales manager. In their former roles, each of these people met the criteria for success. When they were promoted to management positions, however, the rules of the game were changed; in fact, each person had to play a new and different game. Thus, the entrepreneur or business originator must learn to make the transition brought about by growth. But what is required for a successful transition to a growing, healthy organization?

Basically, the small businessman must learn that the best player (himself) is not necessarily the best coach or team captain. Therefore, as the business grows, the small business manager can make his job easier through proper delegation. A willingness to delegate is closely linked to the entrepreneur's personal confidence. Clearly, the owner needs a level of business expertise that permits him to be in control of his business operation and yet be able to draw on the creative ability of the organization's human resources. (See Chapter 11 for a more extensive discussion of delegation.)

Individual decision-making styles often reflect on the small business person's self-image. There is a significant relationship between sound decisions and a successful business operation. The boss need not make all decisions, although some small business owners try to take credit for the sound decisions in order to maintain their good image.

Successful small business managers solicit decision input from employees, and they also rely on the judgment of subordinates wherever and whenever it is practical. A willingness to rely on others springs from faith in one's own judgment. A small business entrepreneur who believes in his or her own decision-making ability is in an excellent position to rely on the legitimate judgment of others. Like delegating responsibility, it is a way for entrepreneurs to demonstrate maturity to the members of the team.

2

differences between large and small organizations

THE BASIC DIFFERENCE between large and small business organizations is not one of size. A small business is not a compact version of large business any more than a small automobile is a miniature replica of its full-sized progenitor: it is quite different in design, purpose, and effectiveness. Differences exist in structure, policy-making procedures, and utilization of human resources between small and large organizations. Small and large firms also differ with regard to personnel practices such as selection, training, and development of employees. To understand these differences between small and large firms is to begin to appreciate the real problems faced by the small business person.

Although these differences have always existed, it is only recently that their importance has been recognized. The vast majority of college-trained students have received their formal education in the environment of the large organization, and there are very few college business curricula that have more than sporadic course offerings in entrepreneurship and small business organizations. Today's small business managers have thus combined the theoretical aspects of courses that are oriented to large businesses with the practical experience of on-the-job training (OJT).

This is unfortunate, since the differences between small and large organizations are such that the application of large-organization concepts to a representative small business may border on the ridiculous. Many current texts on the subject of small business management are guilty of this same error. For example, three or four chapters may be devoted to the application of quantitative techniques including model building, economic order quantity (EOQ), and computer simulation. These techniques are vital to almost every large business operation, but not to small business. Most small business owners today have neither the technical expertise nor the money to make these techniques work. More importantly, they do not have the time to delve into these sophisticated techniques, and even if they did, the smallness of their enterprise would not justify the investment of time and money necessary to apply such techniques.

Critical Areas for Small Business

No place to hide

Everyone and everything is important in the small business. There is no room to hide an incompetent person, since every decision is made out in the open or on the firing line. Therefore, a few incompetents may represent a significant percentage of the workforce of a small firm. Nonproductive workers cannot be pushed over into a little-used, out-of-the-way corner because there is no such thing in a business of this size. Incompetent managers cannot be given an office and a secretary and "kicked upstairs" to perform some perfunctory job that has no meaning: there is no spare secretarial help, there are no unused offices, and there is no "upstairs" as defined in the big business sense.

This can provide some very positive benefits for the small company as well. Because there is no place to hide, every employee and manager must be productive and useful to the company. A person will have to leave the organization if he or she cannot do the job. Poor performance cannot be carried as long as it can be in the large firm.

A special variation of this problem involves an owner who is not working properly. Obviously, he or she will not be fired, but there may be serious consequences for the firm. Customers or clients will not long sustain a lackadaisical operation resulting from inept owner behavior; they will simply deal with other firms, and the owner may find himself out of business in addition to being out of a job. So, even for the entrepreneur, there is no place to hide in small business.

Vulnerability to outside forces

Big business can influence its outside environment through a wide range of activities. For example, a large firm can establish a complete office in Washington, D.C., or at the state capital, to lobby for legislation that will be beneficial to the business. Or employees may receive detailed information involving some current situation where the business organization is encouraging them to act or react in a way that will be helpful to the cause. And because of the large number of workers in a big firm, the employees may be able to exert significant pressure on legislators. In addition, the large firm can afford specialized expertise to help it cope with the increasingly complex legal and political environment; the small firm cannot afford this expense.

Small organizations can influence the outside environment in a number of other ways. Collectively, for example, they can form trade associations or similar units to hire legal and political expertise. And even on an individual basis, there are still many things that small companies can accomplish. Small business owners provide the best protection for their companies by being aware of the external forces that affect them. Awareness and involvement can cause action to be taken when necessary, or it can reflect continuing interest in a situation until something is done. However, many times the small business can only watch as the environment changes.

Hiring and keeping employees

Employees are essential to all business operations. Large organizations can afford to hire many and finally choose the best few from the original group. Small business must hire the few who are needed at the beginning and put them to work right away. Big business can provide directed career development through a succession of jobs within the company over an extended period of time. Unfortunately, small business provides most career development after the fact, and those who survive in the business over a period of years have in effect developed their careers.

Both examples are somewhat overstated, but each has a strong element of truth. Career development is a major challenge for small business today, since big companies can offer good employees so many opportunities that it is difficult for small companies to compete. But although small companies cannot in fact compete with the larger firms in the same kinds of careers, small firms can offer different patterns of career development and in this way become highly competitive.

For example, many a good, young employee has started off working for a small company, and after a period of time has become the sole owner of the operation. There is not a president of General Motors, past or present, who can make the same statement. Small companies provide extraordinary opportunities for the person who is willing to work and to take responsibility. This is career development in the true sense of that term—it can even be called the American Dream. This is one instance in which the small firm can exploit its inherent characteristics and capabilities to recruit and retain good employees more effectively.

Training and development

Historically, there has been little or no employee training or development in the small company, whereas large businesses have provided training at almost all levels as an integral part of the hiring and development process. But at present, there is more of an awareness by the small business person of the need for employee training both on and off the job. Again, the expense of on-site employee training is a roadblock for a small business. Local colleges and universities give small organizations an opportunity to skirt this obstacle by providing a combination of standardized and tailored courses for employees. Many such courses focus on the problems of the small firm.

While large firms can afford their own training departments, small firms must often depend on a myriad of outside sources. The small business manager often wants to train employees but has problems in selecting the appropriate methods. Not only is it a question of dollars; it is more importantly a question of strategy, expectation, and selection. Yet employees need to be trained, and skills need to be upgraded.

A small firm's strength is its flexibility. Flexibility means speed in capitalizing on a market or an opportunity. In this world of rapid change it is even harder to train meaningfully, because the skills and abilities may be needed so rapidly that there is not enough time for substantive training. However, the small business does offer immediate involvement, constant feedback on performance, and rapid advancement. These elements can be used as a basis for developing strategies to effectively train and develop vital human resources.

Effective communication

Communication is an area where small and large business organizations are again quite different, but in this area the small business has a definite advantage, and every owner can make this advantage work for him. People everywhere are turned off by the impersonality of large institutions in which numbers replace names. Individual uniqueness and individual ambitions become lost in the monolithic methods of large organizations. Impersonal treatment is excused as being necessary for efficiency, and thereby cost-effective, but in human terms it creates apathy. People like to be treated as individuals. They like to be called by name. They have a strong preference for individual identity, individual treatment, and just about anything that differentiates one individual from another.

Automobiles purchased from small dealerships demonstrate that customers often buy products from someone who will give them personal attention. We all know of the small car dealer who is within a ten-mile radius of at least six large dealerships and outsells them, although the bigger organizations sell the same makes as the small dealer does. Most of the time the small business owner personally greets the customers in his intimate, one-car showroom. The important difference is his ability to communicate with potential buyers. He is friendly with people from the first meeting on. His customers are individuals, and he calls them by name. There is a strong element of sincerity in the way he establishes his personal business relationships.

The blend of businessman, country boy, and sensitive human being comes across in a positive manner. He communicates this initially while trying to determine the customer's needs. From that point his entire presentation is centered on what his organization can do to satisfy those needs. Customer preference, not dealer inventory, is the main focus of the conversation. The point is not lost on many people: even those who don't buy realize his sincerity and interest in *their* situation. It is a refreshing change of pace from the hustles and hassles found in some large dealerships. Another example of the effect of this kind of direct communication is where a small bank, on the basis of a strong personal community identity, gains a larger volume of loan activity than a large institution that has far greater resources. Again, this situation is not uncommon.

This raises the question of how small business people can communicate effectively with people both inside and outside their organizations. Use the example of the car dealer as a guide. The dealer is an effective communicator because he is sincerely interested in his customers and their needs. He is friendly and enthusiastic, allowing the customer to do most of the talking while he himself listens carefully to what is being said to him. His attention at that time is wholly on the customer, not on what he can sell that person next. The same sincerity and direct, face-to-face communication are possible with regard to employees. Personal contact leads to supportive communication and can encourage employees to commit themselves to organizational objectives.

The communications process is not just a matter of sending messages to other people. It is a human process that requires listening, understanding, and empathy.

Holding ability

Small businesses are especially vulnerable to unstable economic conditions and other unforeseen events. They need holding power or tenacity to protect themselves and get through the rough periods. The owner has to provide protection by not overextending his operation financially or in any other way that might put the business in jeopardy. To move slowly but surely and to plan each step might be as good a safeguard as can be expected in a small business. In the small firm, each decision is critical, because there is no bulk of established wealth to buffer poor decisions. Thus, the need for competent human resources is even more important, and it behooves the small firm to use its people as effectively as possible.

Problems of succession

Large corporations were created to correct the potential and real problems associated with succession. For single proprietorships, however, death or disability of the owner can have disastrous implications. An individual's death, no matter how tragic, rarely makes more than a tiny ripple in the operations of a large corporation.

Entrepreneurs often seek replacements who will have similar characteristics to theirs—they want people in their own image. This example of natural selection can hurt the company if the firm has outgrown its founder's ways and now requires different leadership skills. Carbon-copy succession provides a potential restriction for the organization in a growth period. New ideas can be subverted by a company that dogmatically follows the personal traditions established by the original business ownership. But the same people who try to continue an original management style in the face of changing circumstances would not continue to insist that their children wear size 6 shoes if they now needed a size 7½! Yet such a restrictive course is just as painful for a growing business as shoes that are too small would be for a child's growing feet.

Family selection has similar potential problems if the heir apparent is not qualified for a leadership position. History is full of examples of monarchs who had no real positive characteristics for their role as leaders except that they were born into it. Or consider this example. A father sacrificed for many years and built a fine radio and television business for his son to take over. Very early in life, however, the son expressed interest in other endeavors and made it clear that he couldn't care less about the business. The father finally retired and sold the business to one of his son's highschool classmates. Some 15 years before he had bought the business, the classmate had begun to learn the business by working after school. The story had a happy ending for the business, since it was passed from the original owner of some 30 years to a qualified friend of the family who cared about it and was qualified to run it.

But the outcome did not follow the original scenario developed by the founder, since his son did not assume the leadership role.

Management succession is a prime responsibility of top management of any firm. The small business owner is often so involved with present activities that planning for an adequate and orderly succession and promotion is put off until tomorrow . . . and tomorrow . . . and tomorrow . . . . But "tomorrow" soon becomes "today" and if it is not planned for, the result could be chaos. Meaningful succession criteria must be established and utilized. As the organization grows, the management skills and styles that were effective in its infancy may well need to evolve and to be modified.

Succession is not tomorrow's activity—it is today's plan.

Family succession and career path development

Sometimes outstanding qualifications—or the lack of them—do not determine the extent of an individual's success in a small firm. Many small businesses are family-owned, and members of the "royal family" have the inside track to the top positions. In such a company, you may never be able to get to the top. Small companies can and do suffer from this kind of royal succession syndrome. And even if you actually marry into the family with all good intentions, at some point your progress may be cut short abruptly when another member of the family receives the top job, thereby becoming not only your relative, but also your boss. Therefore, before you make any commitment to a small organization, you should plan in detail and make allowances for any of the owner's family members who may halt your individual career path development in that company.

Delegation of responsibility

A significant difference between small and large businesses can be found in the application of delegation principles. Delegation in the large corporation is a way of life. There are too many duties and too many things going on to avoid delegation. In the large firm, the emphasis is on the goods produced and the services rendered rather than on the people involved. In the small firm, the style is more personal (oriented to the particular owner of the business). In fact, people often start small businesses so that they can exercise direct control over the operation rather than be forced into reliance on others. Consequently, delegation is seen as essential to large companies but often appears optional to small business people. But in both cases, failure to delegate can have disastrous personal and organizational consequences.

Established businesses have learned the value of delegation, but small businesses may be doomed to continually relearn (through a series of bad experiences) the lesson of delegation. Wherever they serve, smart business managers know the importance of delegation and of sharing the work responsibility, and they do everything in their power to make delegation work. Yet to the small business person, delegation is not merely a job description phenomenon—it is a very personal process. For the small business manager is not delegating job duties; he is, in a sense, delegating part of himself.

In large firms, the organization can absorb mistakes; in the small firm, if the delegated job is poorly performed, it can sometimes even jeopardize the owner's capital investment. Thus, delegation is difficult both organizationally and emotionally for the small business person, because it seems so much easier to do it himself. But that way a price is paid: failure to utilize the higher-level person's skills in new, challenging, and significant arenas, and a resulting lack of input of fresh ideas into the organization.

Motivation

Another difference between large and small firms is in the area of motivation. This is one area where the owner or manager of a small business can really excel, because in their attempts to motivate people, managers in large organizations are shackled by many conditions such as company policy and tradition, union contract

George W. Rimler holds a B.S. from Poly-
echnic Institute of New York and an M.B.A.
nd D.B.A. from Georgia State University. He
s the author of numerous professional papers
n the subject of business and human
esource management, and is currently Pro-
essor of Management at Virginia Common-
vealth University, where he also serves as
Director, Small Business Development.

However, entrepreneurs are
their employees in any way
flexible and responsive.

rrent to motivation is the
ominant that he discourages
use their enthusiasm. When
ne motivational process, this
business at a far greater dis-
e large organization. This is
all businesses have so many
which are not available to
tivation should be a bulwark
mes it is treated as though it
ent strengths in the area of
be explored and developed.

Neil J. Humphreys received his undergradu-
te training in business at Drexel University
nd received his doctorate from the Wharton
School, University of Pennsylvania. He has
ad extensive personal experience in the
peration of small businesses, and is cur-
ently Associate Professor of Management at
irginia Commonwealth University.

3

Behind an able man there are always abler men.
CHINESE PROVERB

the new employee and
the small firm

Is THE work ethic dead? Do people still want work to occupy as significant a position in their lives as it did for past generations? Although the answer to these questions is still unclear, one thing is definitely known: the views, values, attitudes, and motivational patterns of those who are just entering the workforce are significantly different from those held by their ancestors. The rewards, both internal and external, that were used to gain the commitment of previous generations of workers to the organization do not appear to be working for this generation. Money is no longer enough, praise is questioned, promotions are turned down—all out of a need for "meaningful work experience."

New Employees, New Realities

Perhaps no challenge is ultimately more significant to the success of an independent business than the ability of the small business person to gain the commitment of the new employee. Since the manager must create an environment in which subordinates willingly work toward the organization's objectives, any strain in the relationship between the owner-manager and the subordinate reduces the chance for an effective team. The ability of the small business person to succeed depends to a large extent on how much employees want to exert effort toward organizational goals. Before any attempt can be made to develop strategies for cooperative, supportive, and synergistic effort, a more detailed look at the new employee is in order.

Reserved commitment

The questions one hears more and more frequently these days include: "Why bother?," "Who cares?," and "Does it pay to try?" More and more potential new employees tend to feel that they will have only a limited chance of exerting a major voice in the direction of the firms they join. In fact, the term commitment may itself be an anachronism.

As Terrance Jackson, Chairman of the National Commission on Productivity, noted: "Attitudes toward work today suggest trouble ahead for U.S. industrial production."[1] Statistics support this possibility: between 1965 and 1970, manufacturing output per man-hour in the United States increased by only 10 percent, compared with gains of 40 to 50 percent by European industrial nations and 90 percent by Japan. To quote Jackson again: "Our rates of productivity are so conspicuously below those of other nations that we must take a long hard look at the institution of work."

In analyzing a poll about worker productivity, George Gallup noted: "If an individual is really enthusiastic about his job, he will presumably go all-out and work to his capacity, yet we find a majority of men admitting that they could accomplish more each day if they tried." A poll confirmed his findings:

---

[1] *Management News*, December 1972, pp. 1–3.

Fifty-four percent of the male manual workers surveyed said that they could accomplish more each day. When they were asked how much more they felt they could accomplish, 30 percent said 10 percent more, and 58 percent said 20 percent more. Sixty-one percent of the male white collar workers queried agreed that workers are not turning out all they could. And virtually the same proportion admitted that they themselves could do more each day if they put in the effort.[2]

Thus, the first characteristic of the new employee which the independent business person must deal with is the new employee's tendency to reserve commitment and effort from the organization. It will take more than words to gain their supportive commitment—it will take active policies.

Educational attainment

The new employee is generally well educated. This is really no surprise to the business people as they hear it, see it, and often experience it with their own children. Yet what does it mean in everyday practice? It means that the new employee is more likely to be able to draw on assorted areas of knowledge when asking, "Why?" In addition, the facile, condescending explanation will not work, because skepticism often goes hand in hand with knowledge. The business person will find that power and authority alone are not sufficient to get employees' cooperation. Instead, policies must be defended on their own merit when they are subject to intelligent scrutiny on the part of new employees.

Desire to participate

The new employee demands active participation and input into decisions and policies that affect the work environment. Organizations that don't allow the new employee to be a participant in the decision-making process will discourage the new employee from getting actively involved on the job.

[2] Ibid.

New employees want *true* participation—consultation, feedback, and expression—before the decision is reached. Research has shown that employees' identification with decisions and policies is stronger if those involved in the implementation are also involved in the formulation. The small business person should realize that the new employees' wish to participate is not a threat to his own authority. Rather, it will guarantee that supervisory authority will be used to effective ends and will enhance the employee's creativity. Of course, participation is controlled by two limiting factors: the amount of information available to the employee, and the ability of the employee to use the information "intelligently" in making a decision. Participation means neither abdication nor decision by plebiscite. It means using available resources to their fullest to aid the small business person in establishing and implementing policy.

The new employee's education will generally allow for meaningful use of the data necessary for "intelligent" decision making, and the information explosion may well put pertinent data at his disposal. The desire to participate may well be reinforced by these two new organizational realities.

The "things will get better" complex

Another characteristic of new employees is their expectation that things will get better and better all the time. They have been raised in an age of relative affluence, and believe that if people try hard, the rewards will be theirs. In fact, in this respect—the idea of reward—they may indeed have much in common with past generations. Yet they will work hard only if the work itself is rewarding to them. As Robert A. Duncan of the Shell Development Company states, "They will get their kicks out of the work rather than the money . . . as long as the salary is competitive."[3] Thus, the work it-

[3] *Business Week,* October 5, 1974, p. 79.

self must have intrinsic value. This may be necessary, but not sufficient; salaries must also be competitive.

Because of their preconception that things will always improve, it may be extremely challenging to manage new employees
in an age that includes any prolonged setback to economic and cul-
tural growth. Attitudes and values change, but at a very slow rate.
In a time of economic uncertainty, basic concerns may predomi-
nate, yet the new employee is not economically naive. Economic
rewards are accepted as part of the employer's obligation, but it
takes more than dollars to gain the extra effort that so often makes
the different between mediocrity and success.

More career women

The history of American entrepreneurship has ample illustra-
tions of female contributions. Yet many of these women were
forced to take over firms when some form of family disaster demanded that they assert themselves. The small business manager
must become aware of the increasing importance of women in the
American economic system. Changing life-styles and family patterns give women the opportunity to maintain careers as well as to
attend to family duties. Female talent may well be the area from
which many new employees come. The small business person
should realize that women now expect full opportunity and will no
longer accept artificial barriers to their career advancement.

In addition, more and more women are starting their own businesses to find work in a tight job market, to find freer expression of
their creative and managerial abilities, and to put into practice
their own ideas of how the business world should work. Whatever
her motives, the self-employed woman is an idea whose time has
come. According to the U.S. Census Bureau, in 1972 there were
402,205 female-owned businesses generating $8.1 million in re-
ceipts. That's only 3.1 percent of all businesses, but the number is
growing and, judging from current trends in societal values and

general life-styles, the number will continue to grow. One indication of this new direction is the recent policy of the Small Business Administration, which set aside $100 million in the last quarter of 1977 for loan guarantees to female entrepreneurs. The same amount was also made available during the first quarter of 1978.

Less concern with security

New employees are less concerned with long-run security than their predecessors were. Although wanting to be rewarded well for the work they do, they often feel that they can fend for themselves in the future as long as they remain professionally competent. In essence, their primary security concern is maintaining and improving their abilities. In this way, they can contribute more to the organization and at the same time decrease their dependency on organizational politics. They can contribute freely and independently as long as they are competent in their areas of expertise. Thus, their greatest interest in security may be manifested by the advancement of their own abilities, thereby assuring their ultimate security. In fact, discussion of retirement plans during the hiring process may be totally inappropriate. Instead, an effort should be made to create and communicate comprehensive and active training and career development plans.

Of course, during times of economic recession and uncertainty, new employees may follow the more traditional path. They may well resemble their predecessors and return to a more basic, dollar-oriented philosophy, since the opportunity for work and the need for secure employment may become the most important factors in their lives. But unless there is a prolonged and severe economic slump, new employees' desire for traditional measures of security will lessen.

Increased mobility

Along with the decreased emphasis on security has come an increase in mobility. One only has to think of the number of families who are dispersed throughout the country to realize that their ties to any one specific area have lessened greatly. Therefore, in competing for good employees, the employer should define the geographic area much more broadly than he would have in the past. It is no longer realistic to define the workforce area within the narrow limits of the immediate geographic area, and the small business may well be competing for good talent with firms that are not in its geographic domain. Of course, increased mobility may also be a blessing for the entrepreneur as a source of talented people, and needs can be met on a broader geographic basis than was possible in the past.

Professionalism

One of the overriding characteristics of new employees is their belief in the professionalism of their field, whatever it may be. Arthur Henry, a $25,000-a-year research chemist for Shell Development Company, does in effect speak for his peers. "If my job weren't satisfying and worthwhile, I couldn't handle anything else," he says. "It is very important to me to be good in my field and be recognized as good. Everything else depends on that."[4] This may be an important new trend for independent business people to account for in their management practices. From accountant to zoologist, the basic loyalty may be to the profession, not to the employing organization; the employer may be viewed only as an intermediary. As this kind of professionalism takes hold in more and more areas, employers will have to adapt to very different standards of loyalty than they found among employees in the past.

The independent business person is in a particularly good position to capitalize on this trend, since professional development and participation can come about faster and more effectively in the smaller organization. With an increase in importance of professional contribution and competence, the small organization has a

[4] *Business Week*, October 5, 1974, p. 79.

unique opportunity to gain committed employees. In the small organization, professional competence, development, and loyalty to the organization can be more easily balanced and enhanced than in the larger organization where one must usually follow certain prescribed career path steps before being able to attain a position of respectable professional stature.

Desire for satisfying and interesting work

The Wall Street Journal of May 16, 1973 carried a lead article entitled "Young Managers Today Less Eager to Adapt, So Firms Alter Policies." This article relates that the new employee, who we have already noted is more mobile than his predecessor was, wants mobility to be an available option for him. He rejects transfers and wants a meaningful job task. He is prepared and demands involvement, because he believes that an individual does not attain contentment, satisfaction, and involvement by sitting on the sidelines.

The less formality and greater attention to accomplishment inherent in small business, which provides easier access to the assumption of responsibility, seems to meet the needs of many new employees. The flexibility, independence, community interest, results orientation, and personal nature of small business are definite strengths in attracting new employees to small businesses.

Why the new employee is important

Despite recent unemployment figures, a severe shortage of managerial talent is on the horizon. Peter F. Drucker, noted management authority, recently made the following observations regarding the future workforce:

> Five years out, maximum, we are going to face a *complete shift* to an extreme labor shortage—the baby bust of 1960–61 will begin to shape the workforce with a drop in birth rate of 25% . . . At this 20-year mark we will have a sharp, almost immediate, reversal from our concern about where the jobs are for young people to where are the young people for the jobs. And one had better prepare. It will take all of the next five years to learn how to do the job with fewer

young people . . . and with a need for greater productivity, and for greater job satisfaction. Money will be a very, very expensive and ineffective way to compete in the job market. . . . You will need to provide the thing young people need the most, the young educated ones especially, and get the least, which is . . . *somebody to talk to* . . . also, *someone to spank them* . . . somebody who is not the boss, and yet works with them and that is a most important need that goes unfulfilled today. . . .

Capital, unless there is a depression, is going to be very scarce . . . physical resources are not inexhaustible . . . *our ability to produce will increasingly depend on the yield* of the third basic ingredient which is the *human factor* . . . that yield could be much higher. . . . This is the only area in which this economy can hope to have a really productive future.[5]

The impact of the new employee is emphasized by another important characteristic of the workforce: the group of workers who range in age from 35 to 45 constitutes a fairly small percentage of the workforce. This is due to the decreased birth rates during the depression (and the deaths attributable to the Second World War). The dip in population in the 35- to 45-year range means that as those above 45 retire in the next five to fifteen years, there will be a premium on obtaining adequate replacements. The only source of additional manpower to fill this gap will be the young workers of today.[6] Thus, it behooves management to recognize the values, needs, and desires of the new employee in developing appropriate strategies for productive utilization of human assets.

Contrary to accepted myth, the values of the new employee and the needs of the independent business person are quite congruent. The ability of the independent business to involve the new employee in meaningful work complements the employee's need for that kind of involvement. Although larger organizations have to

[5] American Society for Training and Development, *National Report*, Vol. 1, No. 4, 1973. (Dr. Drucker's remarks are taken from his speech to the annual meeting of the Society.)

[6] David Nadler, *The Now Employee* (Houston: Gulf Publishing Company, 1974), pp. 4–5.

adapt their structures to provide for new employees' basic professional desires, the small firm merely has to be itself. The small businessman, aware of the trends, need not settle for mediocre employees. Since he has so much to offer, he might as well go after the best he can find.

4

Experience is the name everyone gives to his mistakes.
OSCAR WILDE

the proactive vs.
the reactive organization

IN THE SMALLER COMPANY, each decision is significant, because there is usually no cushion of assets or of established wealth to buffer the firm from the consequences of a poor decision. It is not much of an exaggeration to say that in the small firm each decision is critical; indeed, every decision may be fatal—there is little room for error.

Obviously larger firms are not immune from the consequences of bad decisions, and poor decisions inevitably take their toll. But in a large firm, bad seasons, poor economic cycles, and questionable decisions can be absorbed because of the sheer bulk of operations. Thus, the automobile industry can survive a poor season; Post Cereals, the withdrawal of freeze-dried products; Brown-Forman, the White Whiskey fiasco; and Ford, the Edsel. Not that these mistakes don't hurt (they do), but large organizations have enough diversity and magnitude that the chance of immediate disaster resulting from any one decision is minimal. Such is not the case for the small firm.

Proactive vs. Reactive Decision Making

There are two basic ways of making decisions which an organization can follow. One requires initiative, ownership, and foresight on the part of those making decisions. In essence it demands that the decision maker attempt to master his own destiny. It is called *proactive* decision making.

The other way of making decisions is easier, but usually less effective. It is typical of the organization that never has time to do things correctly but always has time to patch up mistakes. It demands little thought or planning but considerable activity. It does not allow firms to master their own destiny. It is called *reactive* decision making.

Outside influences that affect the small firm

The small-business manager is usually well aware of the number of outside audiences that have an effect on the small firm. No firm—especially the small firm—is immune. Some of the outside influences that may impact on a small firm are:

1. Customers.
2. Vendors.
3. Government (federal, state, and local).
4. Trade associations.
5. Community groups.
6. Employees.
7. Stockholders.
8. Partners.
9. Outside investors.
10. Unions.
11. Local, national, and international events.
12. Competitors.

A reactive organization

A reactive organization responds to outside influences in a crisis manner mainly because the organization has failed to anticipate these influences and thereby develop necessary strategies. The small firm that is reactive is one that responds to the numerous pressures that affect it once the crisis has occurred. There are many examples of this kind of firm: the small manufacturing firm that never thought of training new employees until there were so few qualified, experienced workers around that training had to be rushed, expensive, and less than effective; the small retail firm that delayed moving until the neighborhood's demographics had so drastically changed that the firm began losing business; the architect who went his own way, oblivious to the local ordinance requiring new standards in construction.

A reactive organization moves from crisis to crisis like a fire engine that goes from fire to fire: while it's putting out one fire, another is starting up. Just as the fire department could not practice prevention because it was too busy racing from crisis to crisis, so the reactive firm is unable to control its own destiny. It develops its resources and strategy only in response to outside factors—labor trouble, vendor trouble, zoning problems—and in the process cannot afford to satisfy the basic need of preventing crises from arising.

A proactive organization

A proactive organization attempts to control its own destiny by developing strategies that take into account and even anticipate outside influences. A proactive organization essentially tries to shift the direction of influence: instead of being totally influenced by external demands, it attempts to influence the outside world. Of course there will always be factors that cannot be anticipated: the death or disability of a key employee, natural disasters, floods, hurricanes, an oil embargo, a trade war, a wildcat strike, or the introduction of new technology that makes present machinery obsolete overnight. Although change in the outside environment must by nature remain somewhat unpredictable, a proactive firm develops strategies that take account of outside influences and that at least try to let the small firm master its own destiny. Prevention becomes a substitute for running from fire to fire with a bucket of water.

The crisis-intervention approach yields to one of planning and anticipation. Before the crisis even arises, a proactive organization is aware of factors that influence the firm. Therefore, the organization can develop strategies that are cognizant of, and in turn exert influence on, these forces. Thus, the retail firm periodically checks new locations and local neighborhood trends, the manufacturing firm has an ongoing training program, and the architect is aware of new local laws long before they go into effect.

The development of proactive organization action strategies demand both discipline and time. But the alternative is no better: the reactive firm will have to take time to patch up mistakes, instead of taking time at the outset to make sure that the objective was achieved effectively and efficiently.

There are two key steps in developing a proactive firm: (1) an awareness of its benefits, and (2) a desire to improve the manner in which the human resources of the firm are developed and maintained. This will mean making certain important adjustments in the five key dimensions of an organization described below.

The Five Key Dimensions of an Organization: Reactive vs. Proactive

Organization structure

In the reactive organization, the organization structure is rigid. Instead of being viewed as a means toward a given objective, the organization design tends to be seen as an end in itself. An unhealthy regard is held for tradition, and permanent committees and assignments dominate. The role definition or basic function of individuals is narrowly defined, and any attempt to go beyond one's immediate job responsibility is discouraged. The hierarchical chain of command dominates decision making.

In the proactive organization, an entirely different value system, characterized by more rapid change, is followed. Thus, instead of permanent committees that often exist as ends in themselves, temporary task forces are often formed to address specific new issues. These task forces are drawn from those who are best qualified to deal with the specific committee objective. This is essentially a project management emphasis: those selected to serve may broaden their role definition on a temporary basis. Roles are not considered constraints, but instead are thought to be limited only by one's ability. It is not a question of how much authority and responsibility a role should have but rather how much it can afford *not* to have. Although authority is still respected, the chain of command hierarchy is modified by functional collaboration. A manager is not a commander, but rather a liaison person who gets the best out of subordinates and coordinates their efforts with other functions.

Atmosphere

In the reactive organization, the emphasis is on task activity. Functions generally compete with each other for resources, authority, recognition, and rewards. The atmosphere is often cold, formal, and aloof. Competition may be destructive. Employees are never really committed to the system; they just try to *cope*. People are basically considered units of production, and their true uniqueness and creativity are untapped.

In the proactive organization, the emphasis is on results. Employees are given the freedom to function within established and well-defined boundaries. They can use their own initiative, creativity, and ability to achieve results, rather than being programmed to follow the boss's methods. Managerial decision making and development are not viewed in terms of a production line; the environment is people-centered, warm, informal, and intimate. The positive aspect of competition still exists, but the dysfunctional elements are purged. Resources are still limited, but are budgeted on a rational problem-solving basis. Because the organization is people-centered and caring, commitment is high. People begin to see the big picture because they are aware of other areas and of their unique contributions, and because people really care. The personal alternative encourages organizational success.

Communication

In the reactive organization, communication is characterized by a one-way flow of information—from the top down. Communication is restricted, and feelings are repressed or hidden. Information and trends often take top management by surprise—they are out of touch with the message from those most involved. Communication is one-way, either because higher management levels actually fail to listen and to respond to upward-flowing communications, or because lower levels perceive that this is the case and stop communicating. Regardless of its real cause, one-way communication is deadly: it brings out reactive elements and discourages proactive forces. Often higher levels of management do really listen to the lower levels, but if the lower levels are not made aware of it, all will be lost.

In a proactive organization communication is three-way: upward, downward, and lateral. Higher levels listen and make sure that those to whom they listen know it. A viable two-way communication network built on trust and openness exists between levels in the hierarchy, so that people are not afraid of communicating the bad news as well as the good news to higher levels. Thus, proactive strategies can be developed before a crisis emerges, because top management is aware of potential problems. Feelings are openly expressed and discussed, and people are not afraid to speak frankly and to express their real views.

Communication flows not only upward and downward, but

also laterally. Information is shared by various functions, and both production and sales, for example, realize and appreciate each other's contributions. Indeed, each function recognizes its dependence on the others, and information is freely shared. Other functions within the organization are no longer the enemy, because mutual trust allows information to be shared and discussed so that more effective strategies can be developed for the total organization.

Decision making

In a reactive organization, decision making is characterized by high participation at the top, but low participation at the lower levels. There is a clear distinction between decision making and execution. Indeed, implementation is often thought of as a process that begins after the decision has been made. The decision-making system is quite legalistic in nature, and decisions are usually treated as both final and infallible. The proactive organization has a different view of decision making. First, it holds that decision making requires the participation of all who are affected by the decisions. Although this does not mean a mass plebiscite all the time, it does imply that those participating (a) can deal with the pertinent data, and (b) have enough "intelligence" to interpret the data effectively.

The proactive organization also recognizes one other reality: commitment for implementation is gained during, not after, the decision-making process. Therefore, a premium is put on open, honest, forthright involvement. Implementation is not made effective through degree, but rather through considered input. Thus, the proactive organization can tackle the unknown and can develop original comprehensive strategies instead of mediocre knee-jerk responses. If commitment is not obtained in the decision-making process, if it is nonexistent when the decision is reached, it cannot effectively be demanded at later stages of the process. The proactive small business manager spends little time trying to arouse the workers' commitment after the fact—commitment arises in the process itself. Decisions are not treated as totally final, but rather as hypotheses to be tested, evaluated, and even redirected. Instead of using a legalistic decision-making mode, the proactive organization develops a problem-solving mode in which true issues are analyzed.

Management and philosophy

In the reactive small firm, management's basic value is control—errors are to be prevented at all cost. Of course, this leads to low risk taking and low tolerance for ambiguity. In essence, then, only the concrete is dealt with; the imaginative, the new, or the unknown is avoided. People are factors of production, and are easily expendable and replaceable. Little is done to develop and train human resources.

Quite the opposite is the case in the proactive small firm. Rather than being used to repress and control, power is used to support. Thus, instead of being cautious and low-risk, the firm evolves to the point at which it can take reasonable risks. Errors are not thought of as out-and-out failures; they are seen as learning experiences and a basis for future improvement. The organization is not necessarily one big, happy family, but rather a trusting, supportive, interdependent entity. Workforce planning thinks of tomorrow's needs and recognizes that people planning needs significant lead time. People are seen as key assets to be developed. Because of the supportive environment, strategies and insights are shared between individuals and departments. The organization can take the initiative in developing strategies, because reasonable risks are not discouraged, experimentation is not condemned, and support is prevalent. Individuals are free to take the lead rather than merely to react to crises.

In order to be effective, the small firm must be proactive. Of course, unanticipated and unplanned situations will arise: a flood, a tornado, a fire, the death of key people. But the proactive firm will have already acquired adequate insurance and it will have developed additional manpower. A proactive, results-oriented, action philosophy cannot prevent the unexpected, but it can decrease the number of unexpected outside influences on the firm and it can develop contingency plans for other unexpected events. In order to capitalize on its inherent speed and flexibility, a small firm must be proactive, but it can only be proactive if the human resources in the firm are developed and coordinated.

5

If you treat a man as he is, he will stay as he is; but if you treat him as if he were what he ought to be, and could be, he will be that bigger and better man.

GOETHE

effecting and implementing positive change

ALTHOUGH THE REASONS for the eventual failure of established small firms may be numerous, most failures have a single cause: an inability to change rapidly enough to remain effective in a dynamic environment. Similarly, the newly formed firm may well find that it cannot respond as rapidly to external needs as it would like to and that the end result is failure. Of course change has to be planned and paced. In its highest form, strategic change is the dynamic planning and implementation of proactive strategies and not the willy-nilly, hurried, crisis response. If a small organization cannot use its inherent flexibility, if it suffers from an inability to meet changing needs, it won't survive. New needs on the part of customers present tremendous opportunities for the small firm. The only constant in the organization's environment is change. We need not look at ancient history books to realize the opportunities inherent in changing needs.

Change leads to opportunities for the small firm, whether the change reflects good things for society or not. A recession may lead to fewer sales of new cars, but it might also increase automobile repair shop volume as people hold on to their cars longer. A building slump may hurt many areas of the economy, but the sales of home improvement firms may boom as people decide to make improvements in their current homes rather than move into new ones. A rise in the crime rate may increase the market for crime prevention devices.

A changing environment is necessary for business survival. Change creates new needs, new markets, and new demands. Be it in retailing or in professional services, the small firm must be ready to respond to, and even to anticipate, change. As Table 1 shows, change is indeed all around us in the economic environment.

Often the biggest obstacle to implementing positive change efforts in the small firm is the small business manager. By interpreting change inputs as criticism, the small business manager may well inhibit his or her employees from stating their views on the needed change. Similarly, the small business manager's actions in trying to implement change efforts may well turn off those whose support is necessary for the change to work. More than any other single factor, the manager's attitudes and actions influence the change strategy, its reception, and its implementation. With this in mind, let us look at the real reasons why people resist change, and the small business manager's role in affecting change. We will then describe some approaches that will enhance the chances for successful change efforts.

Why Individuals Resist Change

Individuals resist change for basically one reason—fear—although that fear can take many forms.

Fear of the unknown. Here an individual is afraid of venturing into new waters, and is comfortable with the status quo. This is

TABLE 1. The changing economic environment.

Workforce	1920	1970
Mining, manufacturing, construction	35%	31%
Service (trade, personal, government)	40%	65%
Agriculture	25%	4%

Occupational Shifts	1920	1970
White collar	25%	50%
Blue collar	40%	36%
Service	8%	13%
Agriculture	27%	3%

Demographic Shifts	1920	1970
Place of origin	Foreign-born or recent migrant	Third-generation American
Median education	8.6 years	12.2 years; 1/6 college graduates
Experiences with economic depression	Accepted as normal	Less than 10% have experienced
Percent of women in workforce	Few	40%
Women's attitude about work	Worked only until marriage or birth of first child	Career-oriented

Current Position of Small Business in Economy
500 largest concerns in manufacturing = 14.3 million employees (75%)
 50 largest concerns in retail = 2.4 million employees (20+%)

BUT

95% of all businesses are small by SBA definition
43% of all GNP is contributed by small business
57% of all patents come from individuals and small businesses

commonly expressed by statements like, "Why make waves?," "Things are going pretty well around here," and "We are much better off than we used to be." Any change is risky, and a certain amount of satisfaction in the present situation is necessary for a business to do well. Yet the criterion for satisfactory performance should be based not on what was, but rather on what could be. Individuals learn very rapidly to give the boss what he wants, and if he demands little in the way of positive change but instead rewards compliance with the status quo, that is what he will get from employees.

Fear of failure. No one likes to fail. Yet failure should not be the end of the change process. Rather, it should lead to a thorough analysis of where we went wrong, why, and how we can prevent failure next time. Yet certain organizations have value systems under which failure is synonymous with death. Often this value is held by the small business manager despite the numerous studies that have shown that most successful entrepreneurs seem to have the ability to rebound from failure, even failure severe enough to cause business closings and personal bankruptcy. The small business manager should not hold different expectations about failure for his employees than he does for himself. Just as he has learned from past failures, so can his employees.

Failure should be viewed as a learning process. Of course, only appropriate risks should be taken and success should be expected—but if one cannot afford to fail, one cannot afford to think or to do anything differently. The small business manager must realize that fear of failure leads to resistance to change, and must then act accordingly. Thorough discussion, a wide-ranging review of alternatives, and commitment to the jointly developed strategy plan may lessen the fear, but the best way to deal with it is to view failure as an expensive, but sometimes necessary, learning experience.

Fear of changes in social environment. Many good technical changes, designed by brilliant engineers, have been sabotaged because the accompanying changes in the social environment were never considered. Thus, the decision to vary work hours may make a lot of sense on a production and cost basis, but to those affected by the change, resistance may arise because of social factors—a change of work station, car pool members, lunch time, or even break time—and because of the fear of a new, unknown social situation.

Fear of economic consequences. Change involves economic uncertainty. New processes, new products, and new organizational settings may well evoke economic fear. Although the real economic fear *should* come from lack of change (for this inevitably results in stagnation), the fear of dire economic consequences is so strong that it raises resistance to change, especially if the economic environment is already shaky. The small business manager should also realize that the economic issue is always high in the value system of the employees even though they may not voice it (which may reveal that it's much too important and personal an issue to discuss idly).

Fear of decreased job security. Another important factor in resistance to change—and related to the fear of economic consequences—is the myth that we are all expendable. All jobs require skill and knowledge, and employees should be made aware of the importance of their contributions. This is one of management's most critical tasks. Yet the issue of job security must be recognized if resistance to change is to be overcome. Here again, the fear is seldom directly expressed, but instead takes the form of a mental block that thwarts change. Of course, some changes do involve layoffs, but they are by far the exception: most change involves challenges that may well lead to new growth opportunities. This must be explained to all members of the small firm, and the competency of new employees should be recognized, appreciated, and reinforced.

Fear of additional work. Another reason for resistance to change is the fear on the part of the employees that the net result of the change will be additional work duties. Surprisingly, this concern is often related to the amount of work, rather than the type of work. Sometimes additional work can be a blessing in its variety and potential for growth. But the fear of additional work is often reinforced by unpleasant past experiences under similar situations. The small business manager should allay the employees' anxieties about this by guaranteeing that any additional work volume, duties, or responsibilities will be recognized and compensated.

Fear of criticism. We all like to think that what we are doing and the way in which we are doing it is well respected and received. Indeed, the initial reaction—perhaps subconsciously—to the thought of change is often defensive. Doing something differently, taking new actions, and generating new alternatives are all departures from the present. The present is the very thing that we control, and big changes in it can be interpreted as criticism of our efforts. Resistance to change may well arise because change is interpreted as a criticism of the present. The small business manager should be aware of this kind of fear and the resulting resistance. Change should be seen as a positive effort toward achieving all that the organization is capable of achieving rather than as a criticism of past or present performance.

How the Small Business Manager Can Contribute to Employee Resistance to Change

One of the unique characteristics of the small firm is that the attitudes and values of the key individuals are usually known to all. Fewer management levels are there to filter the views of the top people. These views are known and can be a key factor in aiding or aborting change efforts. Sometimes the views of top management are key factors in determining the effectiveness of change efforts (new ways of doing things) in a small firm. In fact, since it has the final veto, top management often determines whether change is necessary. Because of this more direct influence, top management in a small firm can have a powerful impact on whether employees accept or resist change. Perhaps a good starting point is to look at some of the ways small business managers can inadvertently contribute to employee resistance to change.

By viewing change as criticism. Just as the employee may look at a departure from the status quo as an implied criticism and may therefore resist change, a similar value system may be held by the small business manager. If this is the case, change will not be pushed from the top and few recommendations for change will come from employees, because an atmosphere will develop in which necessary innovative ideas are not expressed. Inevitably this will lead to loss of interest and commitment by employees and will negate the chances of change efforts originating at lower levels. The small business manager becomes an obstacle rather than an ally: he must be worked around rather than with. The highest value becomes polite appeasement, and nobody pushes the issue, so the needed change is left to die on the vine because the boss interprets this kind of initiative as a criticism. Thus, necessary changes never occur, and the employees do their jobs but not one bit more.

By failing to be specific about change. Change involves uncertainty, and the less specific information provided to the employees, the more worry, anxiety, and general unrest will result. Lack of specific information allows the mind's worst suspicions to become credible. A shift change may be viewed as a major layoff, and a production change as a plant closing. *Be specific*—tell employees who is affected, how, when, why, and in what manner. Remember, not dealing with specifics encourages doubt and resistance. As the small business manager, you must anticipate the specific concerns of those involved and address those concerns.

By failing to allow those affected to be involved in planning. Research has demonstrated that the chance of successfully implementing change increases significantly when those affected by the change are involved in the planning of it. Involvement should come in the stage prior to decision making, and should be encouraged at each point in the planning process. Involvement in the planning process joins all concerned in building together with a constructive purpose and direction.

By failing to keep employees informed about a change. Even those small business managers who invite participation are prone to make mistakes in this area. Constant information about change must be supplied to all affected—even those who appear to be indifferent. If not, the impression will spread that management is "doing nothing." Progress reports should be made, preferably in as open a manner as possible. It is not enough to do—others must know what is being done.

By not realizing his impact on change. We remember the case in which the owner of a retail outlet casually remarked to some employees that "some of the shelves look dingy." To the employees this was a signal to change something, and that is just what they did. The manager, who was trying to please the owner, had a few people work overtime the rest of the week to empty, clean, paint, and then restock the shelves. To his surprise, the owner had arranged to have an outside contractor replace the shelves on Sunday. The manager was shocked to realize Monday morning that all of the overtime work was in vain, because the shelves had been replaced. The owner had not meant this to be a criticism but was merely stating his view of the situation and wrongly took action without proper communication. Any authority figure in a small firm must recognize that his or her most casual, most innocent remark may be perceived as a direct command and could trigger attempts at change, which are often wasteful, unplanned, and unsuccessful.

Overcoming Resistance to Change

Resistance to change may not be inevitable, but it does occur very often. This resistance is frequently caused by the employee's past experiences with change, which may not have been very favorable. Although many changes (such as promotions, pay raises, and the introduction of new product lines) can offer greater opportunities, people may still resist those changes. The small business manager must be aware of this potential resistance, be sensitive to it, and take action to overcome it.

Tell the employees how the change will affect them. The first questions a person asks upon hearing of a contemplated change are: "What's in it for me? How does the change affect my salary, security, work duties, work hours, and so on?" These questions must be answered immediately. If they are not, doubt will give rise to anxiety, and the worst possible scenarios will be imagined. Put yourself in the other person's shoes. Charts, graphs, earnings projections, and sales per man-hour requirements are all important, but all have nothing to do with the first needs that should be addressed: "How does it affect me personally?" and "What's in it for me?" Once you have been able to allay people's fears about those problems, you can present them with the hard, objective data.

Involve the employees in planning the change. Resistance to change will be less intense when those to be affected, or those who believe they might be affected, know why a change is being made and what the advantages of that change will be. This can be done most effectively by letting them participate in the actual planning. Besides helping them to understand the when, what, where, how, and why of a change, participation will ease fears that management is hiding something from the employees. In addition, participation can stimulate many good ideas from those who probably are best acquainted with the problem that necessitated the change in the first place. It also alerts the small business manager to potential problems that might arise when the change is implemented. Commitment to implementation should come in the planning phase, not after the decision has been reached.

Provide accurate and complete information. When workers are kept in the dark or are given incomplete information, rumors start to spread. This creates an atmosphere of mistrust. Even when the news is bad, employees would rather get it straight and fast than receive no news at all. Lack of information makes them feel helpless, while the whole story—even if it's unpleasant—at least lets them know where they stand.

Give employees a chance to air their objections. Change is more easily assimilated when the small business manager provides an opportunity for feedback that may reveal unsuspected reasons for opposition to the change. Change may often disturb work factors ancillary to the basic purpose of the change. For example, an attempt to increase production may cause a shift in employee work stations. In such situations, the manager may very well see the logic of the hard-cost figures and engineering reasons behind the decision, but employees must still be allowed to air their objections candidly. Otherwise, their resistance may sabotage the change, and the manager may never become aware of the real reason for the failure.

Technical change has social and personal consequences, and these must be accounted for if change is to occur smoothly. In making any change, managers should take group norms and habits into account. They should ask such questions as, "Will the change break up congenial work groups? Will it disrupt commuting schedules or car pools? Will it split up long-standing luncheon partners? Or will it require temperamentally incompatible employees to work together?"

Make only essential changes. Most employees can tolerate only so much change. When they are confronted with many trivial or unnecessary changes, their reaction will be irritation and resentment. Even more important, they will be less receptive to major changes when those are required. People will support change if they understand the need for it, know their role in it, and are aware of your expectations. Change does not imply a freewheeling organization in a constant state of confusion, but rather a well-knit team that advances strategies effectively. Change for the sake of change is a waste—for everybody.

Learn to use problem-solving techniques. Research in behavioral science furnishes some useful guidelines in solving problems that arise from implementing change. First, identify the real problem. The small business manager may think, "If I could only get Mary to retire, the morale of the group would improve." But deepseated attitudes rarely are caused by a single individual in a group. Secondly, be aware of timing. It's much easier to influence people favorably toward new data processing equipment before it's installed than afterwards. Third, help people solve problems to their own satisfaction. They will react negatively to such advice as, "You shouldn't take that attitude," or to attempts at persuasion like, "I'm sure when you have all the facts, you'll see it my way."

Adjusting to change is difficult enough under the best of conditions. The small business manager can make it far easier for his subordinates—and for himself—by taking these positive steps to forestall potential resistance. (See the Appendix in the back of the book for a series of questionnaires that will give you a chance to look at the nature of change and its effects on your organization.)

6

The worst cliques are those which consist of one man.

G. B. SHAW

developing trust and openness in the working environment

WHEN ALL IS SAID AND DONE, the key factor that differentiates the successful small firm from the 95 percent that fail is good management. A manager is usually thought to be someone who accomplishes objectives through the efforts of others. However, the definition sometimes implies a subtle manipulation of subordinates. An effective small business manager is one who creates an environment in which people working together in groups can realize their full potential in pursuit of common objectives. This is a far more realistic role for a manager than the role of a manipulator.

Organizational Climate

Just as individuals have personalities—attitudes and values influenced by the totality of an individual's experiences—so do organizations, ranging from one of synergistic cooperative effort to one of suicidal self-destruction. Organizational climates likewise reflect the full range of experience of the organization. In the small firm, an additional variable plays a key role in shaping the organizational climate: the personality and values of the small business person.

The organizational climate is the main ingredient in unleashing or inhibiting the human potential of those involved in the small firm. The climate of a small organization is best revealed by what happens when the manager is not around: do employees go out of their way to solve a customer's problem or do they merely go through the motions? In essence the climate reflects the values and norms of the organization. For example, if the boss comes back from vacation and has to deal with a multitude of routine problems that have accumulated during his absence, it indicates a lack of competent employees who can take action on their own. Compare this situation with one in which the organization runs smoothly during the boss's absence: each organization has a completely different climate.

Creativity

Creativity is everywhere and in everyone. We all have the capacity to invent new ways of doing things, to give old routines new life, to see our lives and our jobs in new ways. Creativity exists at all levels: even the most mechanical, routinized job demands a certain amount of creativity, although admittedly its range is extremely limited. Unfortunately too many managers downgrade the potential for creativity in the people they supervise, and suppress the aspirations of their employees for at least a modicum of individuality and self-expression. Frustrated and discouraged, employees often abandon any attempts to be creative and instead retreat into cynicism and a glum fatalism. It becomes a self-fulfilling prophecy: managers who see their employees as uncreative people often create circumstances which will virtually guarantee that those people become uncreative.

But when creative energies do not find positive outlets for expression, they can often become destructive. Stubborn resistance to managerial directives, indifference to the work situation, attempts to pass the buck—these are some of the behaviors carried out by workers whose creativity has been thwarted. All of their ingenuity goes into shirking responsibilities and making excuses, the sheer inventiveness and originality of which can be staggering! Small business managers can prevent this from happening by encouraging employees to be creative and by channeling their creative energies in a positive direction so that employees, managers, and the organization itself will benefit.

The Small Business Manager's Views of People

The organizational climate is colored by the small business manager's views of people. Generally these views can be divided into two categories—X and Y. This is not to imply that X is bad or Y is good; the terms X and Y are merely classifications. Another point worth noting is that the X and Y classifications merely reflect the small business manager's *assumptions* about people. These assumptions are formed from past experiences—personal and organizational—and the manager's actions follow from these assumptions. Here are the basic characteristics of Theory X and Theory Y. (To see how your own attitudes fit in, answer the "Management Attitude Questionnaire" in the Appendix.)

THEORY X: The traditional view of direction and control.
1. The average human being has an inherent dislike of work and will avoid it if he can.
2. Because of this characteristic, most people must be coerced, controlled, directed, and threatened with punish-

ment to get them to put forth adequate effort toward achieving organizational objectives.

3. The average human being prefers to be directed, wishes to avoid responsibility, has relatively little ambition, and wants security above all.

THEORY Y: The integration of individual and organizational goals.

1. The expenditure of physical and mental effort in work is as natural as play or rest.

2. External control and the threat of punishment are not the only means for bringing about effort toward organizational objectives. People will exercise self-direction and self-control in the service of objectives to which they are committed.

3. Commitment to objectives is a function of the rewards associated with their achievement.

4. Under proper conditions, the average human being learns not only to accept but to seek responsibility.

5. The capacity to exercise a relatively high degree of imagination, ingenuity, and creativity in the solution of organizational problems is widely distributed in the population.

6. Under the conditions of modern industrial life, the intellectual potentialities of the average human being are only partially utilized.[1]

Again, remember that X and Y are merely assumptions about people, and the actions follow the assumptions. Thus, X develops an organizational climate that is based on fear and control. Since people are basically dumb and lazy, control is the key, because if controls didn't exist, the worker would goof off. The organizational climate puts a premium on control. Organizational climates that emphasize control are often captives of those being controlled.

[1] Douglas McGregor, *The Human Side of Enterprise* (New York: McGraw-Hill Book Company, Inc., 1960).

Control systems take time to develop and implement. They also cost money both in terms of actual dollars spent and in terms of future opportunities and efforts foregone because the organization was too busy controlling its present actions.

But the real problem in control systems is less apparent: the organization is often dependent for the actual data measuring performance on those who are being controlled. The expense voucher, for example, is supposed to be a means of controlling employees' expenditure, but since the employees themselves provide the data, they can easily pad their bills. Thus, too much emphasis on controls can result in employees' devising ways of beating the control and even sometimes slowing down output to sabotage the control.

There is a story about an engineer for a small firm who was asked by the boss to visit a vendor for a five-day quality-control fact-finding mission. The engineer, who had not traveled very much and was therefore somewhat apprehensive, asked the boss what the weather in the vendor's city would be like. The boss answered him that the days would be nice and sunny; the nights, cool and balmy. The engineer left and, accepting the boss's words as the truth, took neither an umbrella nor a coat. When he arrived at his destination, the engineer was shocked to discover that the climate was not warm and sunny, but was instead cold and drizzly. After three days of this weather, the engineer purchased an umbrella and raincoat at a cost of $64.79.

Upon his return, he included these costs in his travel voucher, which totaled $412.19. The day after its submission, the voucher was returned with red lines through the expenditures for the raincoat and umbrella and a note saying that personal expenditures were not reimbursable. The engineer resubmitted the voucher without itemizing the umbrella and raincoat. The revised voucher still totalled $412.19, but this time the engineer attached a note which said, "The umbrella and raincoat are in there somewhere. You find it!"

The Theory X and Theory Y model gives the small business

manager a framework for evaluating his or her assumptions about people. The specific situation may well determine which set of assumptions is most valid. Theory Y action does not mean abdication of responsibility; it demands work-oriented objectives and requires the small business manager to play a supportive role that helps unleash creativity and self-control. Yet the small business manager may often find it more difficult to manage in a Theory Y orientation than in a Theory X framework. If a Theory Y approach is used, the manager is often robbed of his biggest weapons—fear and coercion. It is more difficult and demanding to manage motivated, committed, and independent individuals than it is to manage people who are reduced to the status of beasts of burden.

Trust and Openness

Trust and openness among individuals in the small firm is essential if the firm's management team is to be effective. Many firms, large and small, suffer from a disease we like to call "departmentalitis." This disease occurs when each department or function views itself as the most critical. For example, finance, production, and marketing are essential, no matter what kind of business you're involved in, but although each is important, none is dominant. Lack of trust and openness prevents the sharing of information and the resolution of issues between various functions. But it must be realized that each department is not in a world of its own, that all are part of the same team, and that effectiveness demands cooperation from everyone.

One symptom of departmentalitis is that each department views the other as an obstacle that must be overcome. Indeed, in advanced cases of the disease, so much effort is needed to overcome internal obstacles that little is left over to fight the real competitors. Management of the small firm is often aware of this condition, and uses terms like "personality conflicts" and "lack of interdepartmental cooperation" to describe the situation. In reality, of course, the disease stems from poor teamwork characterized by a lack of trust and openness between individuals and functions.

A manager can preach the necessity of having his people level with him and with one another, but words are not enough; trust comes from past experiences with various individuals and continues to grow as the benefits are realized and the objectives are reached. Trust and openness cannot be developed unless there is a commitment toward enhancing the workings of the management team. Nor can they be developed without taking risks and possibly modifying one's views.

The Role of Conflict in Organizations

Most of us have grown up thinking that conflict among people in the same organization is bad. We have also been taught that it is wrong to become "personally involved" in organizational issues. Statements such as "John, you're getting too excited about this," and "let's keep personal feelings out of this" illustrate the belief that conflict is bad and that organizational decisions should be made objectively. However, conflict can be a very effective tool in helping to develop trust and openness. More importantly, conflict is natural. It cannot be negated or done away with; it can only be suppressed. But suppressing conflict does not eliminate it—it will still exist, albeit surreptitiously.

The decision that is reached without heated debate and without true discussion cannot win people's commitment. Commitment comes from input, from thrashing out ideas, from emotion and involvement. Is it any wonder that many decisions are poorly implemented? Have you ever been on a committee of, say, seven people where you felt that the minority opinion shared by you and one or two others was not listened to or appreciated? Let's assume that the majority opinion was implemented and a year later you learned that the decision had been so ineffective that the project had been scrapped. Honestly, would your first emotion be joy or sadness? You would probably say to yourself, with some satisfaction, "See, I told them, but they wouldn't listen!" And so, the resentment continues to fester, which only proves this point: conflict that was never expressed does not disappear; it exists below the surface and leads to dysfunctional consequences—low trust, low commitment, and poor communications.

Dealing with Conflict in Making Decisions

Conflict can either be dealt with in an open and constructive manner or it can be suppressed; it cannot be denied. In fact, it is possible to argue that if there is no conflict and thus no disagreement, the people involved in making the decision don't really care very much. Positive conflict leads to enlightened and creative decisions. It develops commitment, and all concerned do not merely *feel* involved—they *are* involved. Conflict is inherent in meaningful decision making. Here are some examples of the various ways in which conflict may be dealt with.

1. *Denial of conflict.* The leader gives his view and asks for comments. Nobody responds and the leader takes this silence for agreement. But in reality nobody agrees or disagrees, because nobody really cares. The past has taught those on the management team that "the boss" doesn't really want comments or discussion; he wants approval. Thus, the conflict is denied.

2. *Minority rule.* The leader voices his view and asks for comments. One or two people agree with his opinion and the leader says something like, "Well, that seems to make it unanimous." This is a modification of conflict denial. Silence is again taken for agreement, but selective listening and railroading denies the true expression of the majority.

3. *Majority rule.* This is a frequently used strategy by small

business managers. It is the democratic way, and conforms to our general election psychology. All members of the management team vote on an issue, and the majority rules. Unfortunately, regardless of what the vote is, the ultimate responsibility for implementation most often remains with the leader. Thus, the small business manager may often espouse democracy and participation but may be put into the role of having to work around its product rather than deal with its output. This confirms the skepticism and negativism of managers on the management team who, because of past experiences, expect to get the shaft when decisions are made and who feel that all the talk of "participation" is an empty exercise.

The other defect of this method is that it tends to degenerate into "getting even next time." If your view loses 4–3, the issue for you is not how to implement the approved decision, but rather how to develop strategies so that next time your "side" will win. You will therefore have less of a commitment to the success of the project, since you will be able to get some satisfaction if it fails and you can then say, "See, I told you so."

Another closely related problem is that under majority rule, conflict is often glossed over in the effort to be on the winning side. What most people agree on is taken for the correct decision, whereas in reality a majority vote says that most people agree on a certain alternative, which does not necessarily make it the best choice. Voting is not bad if adequate discussion and conflict resolution takes place. The potential flaw in voting as a decision-making technique is that the concern is often more with the politics of the decision-making process than with the effectiveness of the output.

4. *Consensus.* Consensus is a slow process: it takes far longer than any of the other decision-making strategies discussed here. Yet it is efficient and effective, generates commitment, and avoids the necessity of patching up mistakes. Many small business people use the first three methods because they don't have the time to use the consensus technique. Yet the same individuals and organizations seem to always have the time to remake decisions that proved inef-

fective the first time around. Perhaps the real ineffectiveness lies in the decision-making process, and if this were improved there would be less need for patching up mistakes later on.

Consensus involves open, complete, lengthy, and even emotional discussion and debate. Each opinion is actively sought out by the leader, and the environment is one of collaboration. Consensus means that everybody comes away from the decision-making process committed to the decision, actively looking forward to implementation, and expecting positive results. It means that all concerned can live with the decision and that an individual may say, "It's not exactly what I would do, but I understand and appreciate the rationale on which it was based, and I can live with it. It will succeed."

Consensus allows the small business person to hear all, weigh all, involve all, and still significantly influence the decision. He or she retains final authority and demands that all those involved actively participate. It may take time, but the management team comes away from the decision-making process confident and committed.

A Word of Caution

Each decision must be analyzed as to its ambiguity, necessity, and speed. The small business manager should not follow only one technique; decisions that need speed to be effective may demand the authoritarian alternative. Yet if too many of those kinds of decisions are needed, it may well say something adverse about the organization's planning ability and proactive initiatives.

The small business manager must diagnose each situation. The strength of a management team depends on its ability to deal with differences. If everyone on the team thought the same way, perceived the same realities, or brought the same values, the team would be weak; in fact, it wouldn't even be a team—it would only be one person duplicated several times. Just as a football team needs differences—some players block, some pass, some run, and some kick—so must a small business management reward, recognize, and value differences.

Effective decision-making processes based on trust and openness allow individual differences to be put to positive use and to generate new alternatives. Yet, just as an orchestral conductor brings out the best from individual players in an attempt to develop a harmonious effect, so must the small business manager bring out the best team effort. Although recognizing the need for individual awareness, participation, and responsibility, the small business manager must also remember that in a great symphony orchestra, no one improvises at will. It is the leader's job to gain the employees' consensus on objectives and to develop strategies and policies through appropriate decision-making techniques accompanied by an understanding of each individual's role and sphere of authority and responsibility.

Factors in Teamwork

There are nine key elements of teamwork that are vital to small business managers trying to reach objectives through the efforts of the management team. These elements are excellent targets for the small business manager to work toward in developing the various subgroups, including committees, staff, and task forces that may be set up to get work done. They are as follows:

1. Teamwork requires the maximum utilization of the different resources of individuals within the group.
2. Teamwork requires the understanding and commitment to the goals of the group.
3. Teamwork is achieved when flexibility, sensitivity to the needs of others, and creativity are encouraged.

4. Teamwork is most effective when shared leadership is practiced.
5. Teamwork requires a group to develop procedures to cope with the particular problem or situation.
6. Teamwork is characterized by the group's ability to examine its internal processes and functioning so as to constantly improve itself as a team.
7. Teamwork will best take place when the climate of the organization is encouraging and supportive of individual effort.
8. Teamwork requires trust and openness in communication and relationships.
9. Teamwork is achieved when the group members have a strong sense of belonging to the group.

As was noted several times before, the biggest single factor relating to team effectiveness is the team leader—the small business manager. The leader's words—and, even more importantly, the leader's actions—are the ground rules that govern the team effort. Although team effectiveness is a mutual relationship, small business managers owe it to themselves to examine their roles in regard to group effectiveness or ineffectiveness.

What the Small Business Manager Should Look for in Team Efforts

In all human interactions, there are two major ingredients—content and process. The first deals with the subject matter of the tasks on which the group is working. In most interactions, the focus of everyone's attention is directed toward the content itself. The second ingredient, process, is concerned with what is happening to group members and between them while the group is working.

Group process or dynamics deals with such items as morale, feeling, tone, atmosphere, competition, and cooperation. In most interactions, very little attention is paid to process, even when it is the major cause of ineffective group action. Sensitivity to group process will better enable one to diagnose group problems early and deal with them more effectively. Since these processes are present in all groups, awareness of them will enhance a person's worth to a group and will enable him or her to be a more effective group participant. In the next few pages we will go through some questions and guidelines that will help analyze group behavior.

Participation

One indication of involvement is verbal participation. Look for differences in the amount of participation among members. Find out who are the high and low participators and why. When there are shifts in participation—for example, high participators become quiet and low participators suddenly become talkative—do you see any possible reason for this in the group's interaction? Examine how silent people are treated and how their silence is interpreted: is it seen as consent or disagreement? Or just as lack of interest? Find out who talks to whom and if there is any reason for this in the group's interactions.

Influence

Influence and participation are not the same. Some people speak very little, yet hold the attention of the whole group; others may talk a lot but are generally not listened to by other members. Try to determine which members are high in influence—that is, when they talk, others seem to listen—and why. Also find out who is low in influence and the reason for that. Keep track of any shifts in influence and look out for group rivalries and struggles for leadership. Gauge the effect of such struggles on other members of the group.

Styles of influence

Influence can take many forms—it can be positive or negative; it can enlist the support or cooperation of others or alienate them. How a person attempts to influence another may be the crucial factor in determining how open or closed the other will be toward being influenced. Here are four styles of influence that frequently emerge in groups.

Autocrats. Autocrats attempt to impose their will or values on others or try to push other people to support their decisions. They often pass judgment on other members and sometimes block action when it is not moving in the direction they desire. Autocrats are always pushing to "get the group organized"—that's a good way to spot them.

Peacemakers. Peacemakers eagerly support other group members' decisions. They consistently try to avoid conflict or to prevent unpleasant feelings from being expressed. Peacemakers are typically deferential toward other group members and avoid giving negative feedback. They will contribute only when they have positive feedback to give.

Adherents of laissez-faire. These people paradoxically get attention by their apparent lack of involvement in the group. They often go along with group decisions without seeming to commit themselves one way or the other. Ostensibly withdrawn and uninvolved, they do not initiate activity but participate mechanically and only in response to other members' questions.

Democrats. Democrats always try to include everyone in group decisions or discussions. They express their feelings and opinions openly and directly, without evaluating or judging others. These people appear to be open to feedback and criticism from others. When feelings run high and tension mounts, they attempt to deal with the conflict in a constructive, problem-solving way.

The small business manager who is skilled enough to identify these various styles of influence can greatly enhance group effectiveness. For example, it may be necessary to slow autocrats down by tempering their desire to ride herd on other people. Or, realizing that peacemakers may not want to contribute in a situation dominated by an autocrat (although they may very well have something to say), the small business manager should keep the channels of communication open and should encourage comments from everyone.

Decision-making procedures

Many kinds of decisions are made in groups without considering the effects of all these decisions on other group members. For instance, some people try to impose their own decisions on the group, while others want all members to participate or share in the decisions that are made. Managers should be on the lookout for people who make decisions and carry them out without checking with other group members.

Other aspects of group dynamics should also be monitored. If the group drifts from topic to topic, is there any reason for this in the group's interactions? Determine if there are any instances of a majority's pushing a decision through over other members' objections, or whether there are any attempts to get all group members participating in a decision (consensus). It's also a good idea to see if there are people who make contributions that do not receive any recognition or response, and to gauge the effect of this on the members of the group.

Task functions

Task functions illustrate behaviors that are concerned with getting the job done, or accomplishing the task at hand. Managers should determine who makes suggestions about the best way to proceed or attack a problem and if anyone attempts to summarize what has been covered or what has been going on in the group. Any requests for facts, ideas, opinions, feelings, or alternatives should also be noted. Try to find out who keeps the group on target and who prevents it from changing topics or going off on tangents.

Maintenance functions

These functions are important to the morale of the group. They maintain good and harmonious working relationships among the members and create a group atmosphere, which enables each member to contribute maximally. They ensure smooth and effective teamwork. Try to see which people help others get into the discussion (gate openers) and which ones cut others off or interrupt them (gate closers). You should always be concerned about how well members are getting their ideas across. Try to determine if some members are preoccupied and are not listening or if there are any attempts by group members to help others clarify their ideas. Another important problem is how ideas are rejected and how members react when their ideas are not accepted.

Group atmosphere

Something about the way a group works creates an atmosphere. But different people may want different kinds of atmospheres in a group. Insight can be gained into the characteristic atmosphere of a group by examining the general impressions held by group members. Try to determine who seems to prefer a friendly, congenial atmosphere and whether that atmosphere is masking an attempt to suppress conflict or unpleasant feelings. Also see who seems to prefer an atmosphere of conflict and disagreement, and whether these people are provoking or annoying others. Ask yourself if people seem involved and interested and if the atmosphere is one of work, play, satisfaction, withdrawal, or sluggishness.

Membership

A major concern for group members is the degree of their acceptance or inclusion in the group. Different patterns of interaction may develop in the group which give clues to the degree and nature of membership. Try to see if there is any subgrouping in which two or three group members either consistently agree and support each other or consistently disagree and oppose one another. Watch for people who seem to be "outside" the group and those who seem to be "inside" and analyze how the outsiders are treated. Body language can be a good clue. Do some members move in and out of the group, lean forward or backward in their chairs, or move their chairs in and out? Under what conditions do they enter or leave? See if you can determine the reasons.

Feelings

During any group discussion, strong feelings frequently emerge from the interactions between members. These feelings, however, are seldom talked about. Observers may have to make guesses on the basis of the tone of voice, facial expressions, gestures, and other nonverbal cues. Take note of any signs of these feelings in group members: anger, irritation, frustration, warmth, affection, excitement, boredom, defensiveness, or competitiveness. Be on the lookout for any attempts by group members to block the expression of feelings, particularly negative feelings. Watch how it's done and if any one person does it consistently.

Norms

A group may develop standards or ground rules that control the behavior of its members. Norms usually express the beliefs or desires of the majority of the group members about what behaviors should or should not take place in the group. These norms may be clear to all members (explicit), they may be known or sensed by only a few (implicit), or they may operate completely below the level of awareness of any group members. Some norms facilitate group progress and some hinder it.

As a manager, you should always try to determine if certain

topics are avoided in group discussions (for example, sex, religion, personal feelings, or the leader's behavior), which members of the group reinforce this avoidance, and why. Find out if group members are overly nice or polite to each other. Are only positive feelings expressed and do members agree too readily? What happens when members disagree? See if there is some kind of filtering process (self-censorship or otherwise) that only allows certain questions to be asked. Ask yourself if questions tend to be restricted to intellectual topics or to events outside the group. Do members feel free to probe each other about their feelings?

Effective group activities are the key to establishing and maintaining an effective and confident management team. Both tasks and maintenance functions are necessary, and an effective manager needs to diagnose group actions and to become aware of their internal processes. Research has shown that teams which are too heavily task-oriented often destroy themselves in their single-minded desire to accomplish their objectives. Similarly, management teams that are too heavily maintenance-oriented eventually fail because of their inability to achieve objectives: the group harmony gives way to despair as the group fails to achieve its goals.

A wise manager realizes that he who controls the process controls the decisions. This has been known for centuries. For example, in the Palace of Versailles the room in which Louis XIV, the Sun King, made decisions and judgments that affected his subjects is built on a slant. This prompts one to ask why such a beautiful structure as Versailles would have such a severe construction flaw. In truth, it is no flaw. The king understood human decision-making processes well: he was short and knew that a king should be tall. To make the process more effective, he "invented" a form of lifts. The room was designed so that he would always be tall, as his throne was on the high side of the incline. Think of this the next time you call a subordinate in for a "frank" chat and sit behind your grand throne-like desk.

Continuum of Leader Behavior

A small business manager's decision-making behavior may cover a vast spectrum. Thanks to a diagnostic aid originated by Tannenbaum and Schmidt,[2] the manager can assess where he is on the continuum. Each style would be the ideal in a specific situation. If a leader smells smoke in a room, should he appoint committees and discuss participative strategies? No! He should yell, "Fire! Everybody out!" The more unstructured the decision, the more the skills of others are needed and the better the case will be for shared authority. But be careful: too much sharing gives way to abdication, and it is hard to regain control. Figure 1 shows the continuum of authority in decision making.

The manager makes the decision and announces it. In this case, the boss identifies a problem, considers alternative solutions, chooses one of them, and then reports this decision to his subordinates for implementation. He may or may not consider how his subordinates will react to his decision. In any case, he provides no opportunity for them to participate directly in the decision-making process, although he may or may not use coercion.

The manager "sells" his decision. Here, as before, the manager takes responsibility for identifying the problem and arriving at a decision. But rather than merely announcing it, he takes the additional step of persuading his subordinates to accept it. In so doing, he recognizes the possibility of some resistance among those who will be faced with the decision and seeks to reduce this resistance by indicating, for example, what the employees have to gain from his decision.

The manager presents his ideas and invites questions. Here the boss who has arrived at a decision and who seeks acceptance of his

<hr/>

[2] R. Tannenbaum and W. H. Schmidt, "How to Choose a Leadership Pattern," *Harvard Business Review*, March–April 1958, pp. 95–101.

Figure 1. Leadership behavior: which style for which situation?

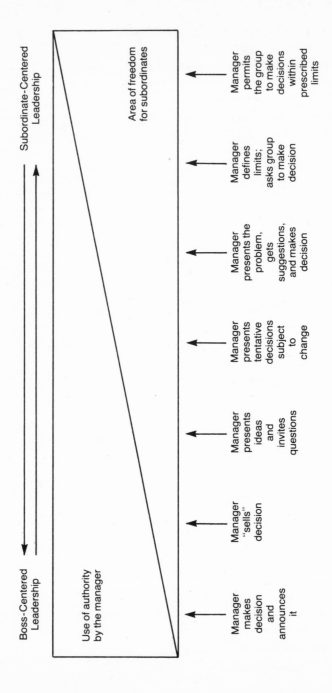

Boss-Centered
Leadership

Subordinate-Centered
Leadership

Use of authority
by the manager

Area of freedom
for subordinates

Manager
makes
decision
and
announces
it

Manager
"sells"
decision

Manager
presents
ideas
and
invites
questions

Manager
presents
tentative
decisions
subject
to
change

Manager
presents the
problem,
gets
suggestions,
and makes
decision

Manager
defines
limits;
asks group
to make
decision

Manager
permits
the group
to make
decisions
within
prescribed
limits

ideas provides an opportunity for his subordinates to get a fuller explanation of his thinking and intentions. After presenting the ideas, he invites questions so that his associates can better understand what he is trying to accomplish. This give and take also enables the manager and the subordinates to explore more fully the implications of his decision.

The manager presents tentative decisions subject to change. This kind of behavior permits the subordinates to exert some influence on the decision. The initiative for identifying and diagnosing the problem remains with the boss. Before meeting with his staff, he has thought the problem through and has arrived at a decision, but only a tentative one. Before finalizing it, he presents his proposed solution for the reaction of those who will be affected by it. He says in effect, "I'd like to hear what you have to say about this plan that I have developed. I'd appreciate your frank reactions, but will reserve the final decision for myself."

The manager presents the problem, gets suggestions, and then makes his decision. Up to this point, the boss has come before the group with a solution of his own. Not so in this case—the subordinates now get the first chance to suggest solutions. The manager's initial role involves identifying the problem. He might, for example, say something of this sort: "We are faced with a number of complaints from newspapers and the general public on our service policy. What's wrong? What ideas do you have for coming to grips with the problem?" The function of the group becomes one of increasing the manager's repertory of possible solutions to the problem. The purpose is to capitalize on the knowledge and experience of those who are on the firing line. From the expanded list of alternatives developed by the manager and his subordinates, the manager selects the solution that seems the most promising.

The manager defines the limits and asks the group to make a decision. At this point, the manager passes on to the group (possibly including himself as a member) the right to make decisions. Before doing so, however, he defines the problem to be solved and the limits within which the decision must be made. One example of this approach would be the handling of a parking problem at a plant. The boss decides that this is something that should be worked on by the people involved, so he calls them together and points up the existence of the problem. Then he tells them:

> The open field just north of the main plant has been designated for additional employee parking. We can build underground or surface multilevel facilities as long as the cost does not exceed $100,000. Within these limits we are free to work out whatever solution makes sense to us. After we decide on a specific plan, the company will spend the available money in whatever way we indicate.

The manager permits the group to make decisions within pre-scribed limits. This represents an extreme degree of group freedom that is encountered only occasionally in formal organizations—as, for example, in many research groups. Here the team of managers or engineers undertakes the identification and diagnosis of the problem, develops alternative procedures for solving it, and decides on one or more of these alternative solutions. The only limits directly imposed on the group by the organization are those specified by the superior of the team's boss. If the boss participates in the decision-making process, he attempts to do so with no more authority than any other member of the group, and he commits himself in advance to assist in implementing whatever decision the group makes.

The management style one uses depends on the particular situation involved. Participation takes time and demands honesty; one-man rule is fast but often lacks support. The manager must diagnose the situation, analyze the risks, and choose the best alternative to solve the particular problems.

7

We ought to do our neighbor all the good we can. If you do good, good will be done to you; but if you do evil, the same will be measured back to you again.

PILPAY

staffing and retaining for results

ONE OF THE GREAT PROBLEMS small business people seem to run up against so often is the very basic question of how and where to obtain good people. Despite fluctuating employment statistics, most small businesses are constantly searching for qualified individuals. Unfortunately, the small business owner is often content with mediocre employees. He has so many things to do that he seldom takes the time to map out a comprehensive human resources plan and often employs people on the spot without much thought about it. When a need arises for an additional person—whether for replacement or growth—an employment agency is rapidly contacted or an advertisement is suddenly placed in the local newspaper. Little effort is spent in planning for the position opening or in developing criteria for filling it.

Manpower Planning

The term *manpower planning* is deceiving in its simplicity. Manpower planning is the culmination of integrated planning and proactive strategy development in all facets of the organization. Manpower planning is basically an attempt to make sure that the human assets in an organization are available in the quality and quantity needed to allow the organization to reach its present and future objectives, and that those human resources are deployed as efficiently as possible.

Many small business managers think that expansion and growth are limited by financial and space considerations. Yet deeper reflection reveals the obvious: buildings can be constructed, stock sold, and loans obtained faster than managers and other key employees can be developed. Many firms find that the real limitation to growth is the lack of adequately trained manpower—and this deficiency cannot be surmounted overnight, since any good training program takes time.

Manpower planning begins with an inventory of present human skills. This is usually done through a survey process. The future skills are also analyzed and noted. Obviously, a great deal of thought must be put into the realistic development of future needs. The differences between present capabilities and future needs are noted, and the data generated this way becomes the basis of training designs and efforts. In essence, manpower planning should answer four questions:

1. Where do we want to go?
2. Where are we now?
3. What additional human skills are necessary to accomplish the objectives?
4. What is the best way for these needs to be met and developed?

Recruiting Good Employees

A concern that traditionally plagues the small firm is the recruitment of personnel. The independent businessman realizes that he cannot afford a massive advertising campaign to attract good people. He knows that the working conditions, location, work demands, pay, and fringe benefits he offers may not match those of the bigger firms. Because of these factors, the small business manager often rationalizes poor recruiting policies by saying, "What can you expect? They sure aren't beating the doors down to work here." The small business manager often settles for less than the best because of the failure to recognize the unique positive strengths of the small firm (see Chapter 10). These strengths are numerous and if promoted correctly, they can become good drawing cards for first-rate talent. The independent business person must make sure that his recruitment strategy exploits the small firm's strengths and does not force him to play the recruiting game according to the big firms' rules.

Interviewing and evaluating the potential employee

Some very important, and in some cases, long-lasting impressions of the organizations are developed in the employee's initial interview. Does the manager take time to really speak and listen to the potential employee? Or are questions sandwiched between phone calls and all kinds of other interruptions? Is the manager direct and concrete, or evasive and flighty? The small business manager owes it to himself, his organization, and the potential employee to realize that interviewing is a two-way process that requires significant skill. He should also remember that as much is communicated by mannerisms and actions as by words.

Time must be taken, set aside, and utilized for employment interviewing. The focus should be on what the person can do now or could do for your firm with some additional training. The most important question to ask when looking for a person to fill a position is: "What are they key results expected from the job?" Until these key areas can be developed and analyzed, little systematic planned recruiting can take place. Other important questions that you will need to ask yourself are:

1. What type of background is needed by an individual to effectively produce the desired key results?
2. How can I tell if the applicant has this background?

Of these questions, the second is usually the more difficult to answer. School grades have become so inflated these days that even other schools view past transcripts with little credibility. And don't assume that the mere possession of degrees guarantees the results you want. The small business manager, often lacking significant formal academic training, frequently acquires degrees more for prestige than for real results.

Another approach is to ask for references from past employers. Although this obviously provides meaningful data about honesty and character traits, it will tell you little about the applicant's ability to do that specific job. First of all, the job you are considering the applicant for is probably somewhat different from his or her previous job, and more importantly, many firms will give exaggerated references to get rid of problem employees. Just about anybody can get two or three good references. This is not to imply that references should not be checked; but they are not the complete answer.

The use—and misuse—of tests

An increasing number of small firms are turning to testing to help gauge the abilities of potential employees. There are a wide range of tests available, from those that judge specific skill competencies to those that measure psychological patterns, such as motivation and determination. Courts have generally held that tests used in selection must test those abilities that are needed to perform the job. This makes it even more important for the small business manager to analyze each job fully so as to distill the essential abilities needed for acceptable performance.

Sometimes testing packages are purchased by the small firm and are administered by the firm itself. Other times the firm relies completely on outside aid in selecting, administering, and evaluating the test and its results. A word of caution is in order: no matter what the test, its validity is dependent on the nature, the personality, and the values of the small firm—and what is valid testing for one firm may not be for another. Just as people have different personalities, organizations have unique traits. This is especially true of the small firm, so many of whose values and views depend on a few key people.

Before a test can give a valid prediction, significant data must be obtained and then related to the environment in which the test is supposed to be predicting performance. Be careful—do not substitute numbers for common sense. It is very tempting to try to remove the uncertainty and difficulties in the hiring process by using test scores as an "objective" basis for hiring someone. Just remember that many famous people—such as Henry Ford, Cyrus McCormick, Alexander Bell, and Thomas Edison, all of whom started firms that have prospered, grown, and contributed materially to society—would probably have a rough time passing present employment tests with the firms they founded! They might well be judged overaggressive, demanding, and egocentric. Testing should not be ignored, but like any other management aid, it should be used wisely. The small business manager must be the master of the test and not the slave of its results. Good management judgment should be used in reaching any final hiring decisions; test results are only additional data to be considered. Testing should never be viewed as a crutch for management judgment.

Where to look for new people

Qualified people take time and effort to find, and in this area the small firm is at a disadvantage. The small firm cannot afford to send recruiters to college campuses. Professional employment service and placement agencies usually prefer to deal with bigger firms. Because they work on a commission basis, these agencies find it in their interest to develop relationships with firms that are able to utilize their services often, and small businesses just don't have as many openings on as regular a basis as large firms do.

Recently the employment agencies of the various states have expanded their scope and efforts. Since this service is free and commissions do not enter into the picture, they can probably aid the independent business person. Newspaper advertisements are expensive, and although they can result in good hirings and gain wide coverage, they may well invite too wide a response. The lack of screening often represents a problem because the volume of responses may overwhelm the firm's ability to handle it.

There is no foolproof way to recruit good employees. The key to effective recruiting is the independent businessman himself. He must always be on the lookout for good people. His own employees will often know of people like themselves who may well make excellent employees. Indeed, the small businessman would do well to periodically canvass his employees, suppliers, and associates in the hope of building a pool of potential employees. The ability of small businesses to recruit effective personnel is too important to be left to chance. The independent businessman should always be on the alert for good talent.

Retaining Good Employees

Although no process can guarantee that all effective employees can be retained by the small firm, certain general approaches are known to work well. The two key variables involved in retaining people are effective evaluation and constructive discipline. Evaluation allows those recruited to know where they stand, and constructive discipline gives them the chance of making improvements where necessary.

Effective evaluation

The term *evaluation* does not usually evoke positive responses. Most individuals tend to think negatively of evaluation because their past history and experiences have been mostly negative. The small business manager, aware of the distaste that evaluation processes usually create, is often wary of evaluating his people. In truth, evaluation is vitally necessary. It is the control that lets us know how we are doing as an organization and how each of us is doing as an individual.

If it is to be effective, evaluation must be a well thought-out, well-timed, and meaningful process. It is necessary for effective performance, yet small business managers often regard it as a necessary evil rather than as a real aid. Evaluation is a sensitive area of human interaction area. It is not the end, but really the beginning, of improved performance.

What to evaluate

Most small organizations use the annual or semiannual evaluation as a standard procedure and policy for appraising performance and determining an employee's merit rating. Few organizations, large or small, are content with the appraisal instrument they use. Sometimes the disapproval of the evaluation instrument is so severe that the evaluation process itself becomes a mere formality.

A typical evaluation form, which can be purchased by a small firm, generally includes "evaluation areas" such as personality, attitude, neatness, punctuality, attendance, cooperation, quantity of work, and quality of work. The supervisor or small business manager is asked to rate the employee in each category. Although the categories mentioned here are quite typical, please note that most of them are irrelevant. An individual could read the newspaper on the job all day, produce nothing, and still receive excellent ratings in 75 percent of the categories! This individual would be most personable; in fact, he would probably have a positive attitude and would be a great ambassador for your organization in the community, saying things like "It's a great place to work." He would always be on time and never absent. (If he were home, his wife might make him do some work around the house.) He would be neat, helpful, cheerful, and cooperative. Of course, he would produce nothing, and therefore the quality and quantity of his work would be questionable. But after all, six out of eight "excellents" isn't bad, and nobody's perfect!

The point is that evaluation must be focused on *results*, not on characteristics or activities. Obviously certain characteristics are necessary if results are to be obtained, yet too much of a focus on traits will jeopardize the evaluation process. Before evaluation can begin, it is necessary for the small business manager to obtain an adequate idea of the key results that are expected.

The evaluation process must be related to the reward system in the organization, and separating it from the reward system is the surest way to make it irrelevant. In a small firm, the owner likes to have his finger in many pies. Nothing undercuts the management team more severely than when the owner makes decisions about rewards and is oblivious to the evaluation and rating of personnel. If this happens, the employees will see the evaluation process as a farce. Proper evaluation is a tool for the management team. It allows each member of the management team a codified, documented record of his people. This record is not a club; it is a coaching device.

Guides to evaluation
Organizations spend thousands and even hundreds of thousands of dollars trying to develop the perfect evaluation form. Save your money—there is no such thing. Effective evaluation depends

more on the company philosophy, communications channels, and general teamwork than on any form. Effective evaluation is a human process, and here are a few guidelines for promoting it:

1. Successful communication of appraisal results depends more on mutual respect and trust than on technique.

2. The problem of appraisal discussion cannot really be separated from the problem of appraisal. A sound appraisal system—one in which both the superior and the subordinate have confidence—is the foundation of the appraisal discussion.

3. The manager must be willing to take the time at the outset to identify the critical requirements of the subordinate's job so that his performance appraisal can be focused on these requirements.

4. The appraisal discussion should center on results achieved in the job—not on the subordinate's personality.

5. Subordinates distrust evasive techniques and procrastination. If a sound foundation for the appraisal discussion has been laid, the supervisor should strive for frankness and candor, rather than worrying about whether he is being sufficiently tactful.

A few additional comments are in order. Appraisal should be a continuing process. Although formal evaluation should take place on a scheduled basis, the small business manager should constantly evaluate his key subordinates, and they should do likewise with their subordinates. When an individual is surprised by the evaluation, it says more about the organization, the evaluation process, and the person doing the evaluation than it does about the person being evaluated.

One question frequently asked by small business managers is: "How can I afford to take the time to constantly evaluate a number of individuals?" The real question is how can you afford *not* to take the time to do this? To guard against the undue influence of events close to evaluation time, the small business manager should keep a record of unusually positive or negative events. This data should be shared immediately with the individual involved, and should be recorded to balance out the impact of events that occur close to the formal evaluation time. The more closely the event (be it positive or negative) is discussed with the individual involved, the better the outcome will be.

Another point worthy of noting is that evaluation should be fair. Fairness means dealing with things as they are; it does not mean praising the good and ignoring the bad. If the small business manager ignores poor performance or hopes the situation will improve without dealing with it, he is making a mistake. Tolerance of mediocre performance leads to only one result—continued mediocre performance. The manager should evaluate his people fairly and accurately. If he overlooks the bad, then he is actually condoning it. Things will not get better unless the situation, no matter how painful, is dealt with. The manager who condones poor performance by "faking" the evaluation in order to be a "nice guy" is really saying to his people, "I'll overlook this poor performance and not deal with it because you are not capable of doing better." People usually know where they stand, and the manager who tells subordinates what he thinks they *want* to hear rather than what they should hear will lose credibility.

Studies have shown that individuals set standards of performance for themselves. Effective appraisal not only evaluates employees but lets them know that the manager is aware of how they are doing. In recognition of these realities, many effective evaluation sessions begin with an employee's self-evaluation, and then they compare this self-administered appraisal with the manager's own evaluation.

Constructive Discipline

The word *discipline* usually generates negative responses from most people. This is, of course, due to equating discipline with punishment; few remember that the word discipline, when used in the sense of "a well-disciplined football team," has very positive connotations. Disciplinary processes in many small firms are often "seat of the pants" style. Discipline often shows management at its worst. It can reveal management to be a disunited, fragmented, uncertain, inconsistent, and hostile group.

But in management parlance, discipline is also synonymous with coaching, teaching, and counseling. In the well-disciplined organization, roles and expectations are agreed upon, and measurements of contribution are understood by everyone and are applied consistently. The well-disciplined organization brings together diverse talents for a common purpose. It is the unity of thought and action in practice.

Discipline in the small firm: the key man

The small firm reflects the attitude of its owner, and, like most other people, the small business owner wants to be thought of in a positive way. After all, he wants to project a friendly and understanding attitude, both inside the firm and within the community at large. As a business prospers and grows, the small business owner becomes more and more divorced from the day-to-day operations of the firm. Other investments, board appointments, and community service positions fill his time. In fact, if he is at all knowledgeable in the delegation process, he should have capable people running the day-to-day activities of the firm, leaving him free for other things.

But because the firm is small, the small business owner is still viewed by many employees as the "man to see." He probably knows all of the employees and, because he tends to be removed from the day-to-day problems of the business, he may have a Mr. Nice Guy image. Therefore, it is natural that from time to time, employees who are having problems may try to bypass their immediate supervisors and tell the owner the "truth" about what's going on. Obviously the small business owner should encourage full and complete communication, yet he must guard against the tendency to undercut those to whom he has delegated authority. It is important for the small business manager to remember that it is not *what* he attempts to do that is important, but how employees *perceive* his actions. If he is not tactful about handling complaints of this kind, it can result in declining morale, decreased initiative, increased skepticism, and lessened commitment by the members of the management team.

Effective discipline demands time. The small business manager should allow adequate time for himself and members of his management team to use discipline as a positive management tool. The greater the number of disciplinary situations that are confronted and resolved, the smaller the number of major disruptive issues that can fester and mushroom into larger and more costly activities.

Indeed, effective discipline demands that disputes be resolved at as low a level as possible. The small business manager should not consider discipline cases as a negative stroke against the supervisors involved; they may well be the most committed and may just be refusing to hide problems. The small business manager who acts chagrined when he hears bad news will modify his employees' behavior so that they don't tell him about problems. Of course, this is not to say that the problems have disappeared—only that they have been kept from the manager. Confronting problems and disciplinary policies must have active and meaningful support from the top.

Characteristics of Effective Discipline

The purpose of discipline should be to prevent the future occurrence of the situation that gave rise to the need for discipline in the first place. Discipline is a form of education that should result in learning. For example, the most effective disciplinarian of all is a hot stove. Anyone, child or adult, who touches a hot stove *knows* not to touch it again. And a hot stove, like most effective disciplinarians, has several key qualities that discourage a person from ever doing the undesired behavior again: the punishment it administers is proportional to the crime; it gives adequate forewarning; its discipline is consistent; it is impartial; and it gives rapid feedback.

Punishment proportional to the crime. The first key characteristic of effective discipline is that the medicine it disperses is proportional to the crime. Thus, discipline is not a set of arbitrary, misunderstood rules; it must be carried out in such a way that the greater the offense, the more severe the penalty.

Forewarning. Adequate forewarning is necessary for effective discipline. Disciplinary actions should not sneak up and surprise anyone. There must be adequate forewarning, so that people are aware that unless they change their actions, discipline will result. In addition, forewarning allows the manager to evaluate and document employees' compliance with directives.

Consistency. Disciplinary policy and procedures must be consistent. The same violation must result in the same discipline whether it was committed at quitting time, lunch time, or in the middle of the work shift. It makes no difference if it is the day before Christmas or the bleakest day in February, Friday afternoon or Monday morning. The discipline must be consistent, and everybody must know what to expect.

Impartiality. Another significant aspect of effective discipline is that it is impartial. Regardless of who needs the discipline, the manager must not pick and choose on the basis of personal considerations. This is closely tied to consistency. There must never be even a hint of a double standard, because if there is, any chance of carrying out effective discipline will disappear.

Rapid feedback. Of all the characteristics of effective discipline, perhaps the most important is the speed of the disciplinary action in relation to the violation. Rapid feedback has several advantages. First, it allows the situation to be dealt with when the facts are freshest and when specifics can be readily recalled. Secondly, it allows the true issues involved to surface. The longer the wait between the situation that gave rise to the disciplinary action and the action itself, the greater the probability that the process will be seen as a personal issue or a vendetta.

The passage of time often makes us forget the facts about a specific situation. Thus, if the discipline session begins with, "John, do you remember the mistake you made two weeks ago?" the receiver of the message (John) won't believe that the problem is too serious. ("If it was so serious," he might legitimately ask, "why wasn't it mentioned earlier?") Since John has forgotten some of the facts of the situation (as has the supervisor), there's a good chance that the issue will become personal. Therefore, instead of dealing with his error to prevent it from happening again, John may wonder, "What does he want from me now?" The more immediate the feedback, the greater the chances for effective discipline. Nothing is to be gained from waiting. Of course, this is not to imply a seat-of-the-pants, half-baked reaction; rather, it implies rapid fact-finding and an immediate response once the basic facts are known.

True discipline should be regarded as a positive management function. Contrary to popular myth, it does not handicap managerial action and prerogatives, but ensures that power, authority, and action are used in a responsible manner. Positive discipline prevents arbitrary decisions and any resulting abuse. It should be viewed as an asset to management rather than an obstacle.

8

training and employee development

THE MANAGEMENT of a small organization, like that of any other organization, must achieve its objectives with the physical and human resources that are at its disposal. The need to replace equipment, to have planned management programs, and to analyze periodically the capabilities of the physical resources is usually a constant management function, but the same cannot be said for human assets. Most institutions, even governmental ones, tend to favor technical over human resources. A new machine can be depreciated and converted into an expense over a recognized period of time, yet investment in a training program for employees must be treated as an immediate expense and must carry with it an immediate reduction in earnings. Thus, small business managers tend to recognize more readily the need for updated and better physical equipment than the need for updated and better human assets. Yet effective human resources is the key ingredient in successful organizations.

Forms of Training

Ideally employee training and development will be a continuing function of the small firm. If training is to be effective, it must be recognized as a long-run fundamental activity—a total effort, not a single "injection" administered to clear up some organizational infection.

Training may take many forms. The simplest and most widely used training approach in the small firm is on-the-job training (OJT). This kind of training is just what its name implies—training that takes place on the job. Usually a senior worker guides the trainee, monitors performance, corrects deficiencies, and evaluates progress. OJT is used for both technical work (such as machinery and painting) and management development and sales activities. OJT is simple, inexpensive, and direct. If the trainer is capable of teaching, it can produce good results. Often the small firm's manager makes the mistake of assuming that his "best" workers should do the training. The results of training depend on interpersonal rapport as well as on technical capabilities. The trainer should know not only the job, but also how to train people.

There are many more complex training approaches than OJT. For example, vestibule training involves teaching the new job in a simulated atmosphere that has been designed to replicate the real environment. A good example of this is point-of-sales training where the cashier becomes familiar with a machine's capabilities through simulated exercises. Vestibule training even carries over to sales training when the salesperson is engaged by an individual playing a specific role and the conversation is taped, analyzed, and discussed. Assessment centers use the vestibule principle in management training. Here an individual is asked to take action in response to various management situations that are presented. The individual's reactions to specific situations are analyzed and rated. Management potential is appraised and deficiencies are addressed. The assessment technique demands a set of basic management

ideas and beliefs—indeed, it requires an effective action management philosophy from the small business manager. If such a framework does not exist, there is no adequate standard of measurement
to appraise an individual's responses.

Some small firms use more formal and more structured training programs. The typical structured program involves the trainee
in the work of various departments, functions, or sections for certain time periods, usually ranging from one to six months. The aim
here is to give the trainee an overall view of the firm and get his or
her inputs about areas of interest. Structured approaches tend to
resemble school curricula: a specific skill or knowledge must be
comprehended before you can advance into a new area. These formal programs not only promote the overall conceptual view, but
they may also be used to develop in-depth specific expertise.

One of the new approaches that is becoming more and more
accepted in the training journals is the concept of organization development. Although organization development seeks to improve
the human functioning of an organization—and this goal unites it
with the older management training approaches—it does involve
some innovative aspects. Basically, organization development aims
at involving the organization or at least entire sections of the organization in human resource development. Thus, the training is designed to deal with realities in the organizational climate which
may affect the acceptance and eventual implementation of new
ideas, strategies, and skills.

Organization development attempts to correct one of the
more serious criticisms of many other formal training approaches,
especially those that involve sending employees off to various
schools, seminars, or institutes. Many formal training sessions present the trainee with new ideas, concepts, and approaches. However, when trainees or participants attempt to apply some of these
new ideas, they are told by their bosses, "That's OK on paper, but
we don't do it that way here." One of the comments that tend to
appear most frequently on training seminar evaluation forms is:

"The session presented some worthwhile new ideas. Too bad my boss wasn't here; then maybe I'd get a chance to use some of them." Organization development attempts to develop chunks of an organization rather than individuals per se, although the two obviously go hand in hand. The hope of organization development practitioners is that by dealing with entire organizational units in the design of the training, more progress can be achieved.

What Type of Training for Me?

The small business manager is concerned with many everyday activities, duties, roles, and responsibilities. In comparison with pressing everyday problems, training may appear to be an activity that can be taken care of tomorrow. After all, today's immediate crises demand immediate attention. But as we all know, tomorrow never comes, and postponing necessary training tends to create future crises. Training must be thought of as a present-day activity to help us accomplish tomorrow's objectives. It is *not* a future activity; it is present-oriented.

Each kind of training has certain advantages and also certain disadvantages which the small business manager must evaluate for each possible action and training strategy. OJT gives those being trained the opportunity for immediate, live involvement. It is adaptable, since new techniques and procedures can be rapidly incorporated into training. Yet its strength may well contribute to its weakness. OJT is prone to haphazard and unplanned efforts. Those in charge of the training may be doing it in addition to their normal duties and may not have the time to do a first-rate job. The trainee, especially if he is new to the firm, may get a feeling of being an intruder and may react accordingly by just going through the motions. All small firms have one OJT program—orientation, be it formal or informal—and the attitudes conveyed through the orientation program may be hard to change.

Vestibule training is not as real as OJT. Because the training is a simulation of reality, the trainee has the opportunity to take flight and sometimes to hedge on his or her commitment to the training effort. On the other hand, vestibule training affords a low-risk, laboratory environment where actions can be analyzed, corrected, and improved. Vestibule training is of particular value in sales efforts.

The "formal rotation" management training program is usually reserved for the middle management level and above. It allows the participants—those who will be dealing with the broader picture because of the level of their position—to develop an overall conceptual orientation toward the firm, as well as a deeper understanding of its specific functions. Whereas the design makes sense, some drawbacks do exist. First of all, today's employees demand involvement, and too long a training program may discourage some of them. Also, those working in the departments where the trainee is temporarily assigned may be operating from hidden agendas. For example, they may recognize that this kind of training is reserved for the "fair-haired boys" and then they may jockey for position with these up-and-coming executives. Thus, the training aspect of the trainees' exposure may be incidental to other desires (such as the desire of many people in the various departments to ingratiate themselves with the trainee, whom they may consider to be the "heir apparent"). Yet rotation may be a good training method if timetables for it can be established and maintained; if the system is designed to give the individual a true view of the organization; and if the program helps develop specific areas of possible individual contribution.

Organization development efforts are not necessarily designed to give a person or a functional unit new skills; they may be designed to affect people who have considerable experience in the position and in skill capacity. Organization development attempts to improve the human functioning of work units and to build cohesive work teams. The gains from organization development efforts can be substantial if top management is behind the effort and thus ensures a supportive climate for addressing issues. But like any training effort, organization development must have recognized objectives and evaluation procedures, as well as an established timetable.

One small business manager had been sending his key people to numerous training programs in an attempt to make them more "sensitive" to the people around them, with whom they would interact daily. This manager was complaining that his people had become so sensitized that he would have to send them to another training program that would desensitize them so they'd get back to work again!

Organization development can get into some unusual avenues and impractical exercises, but if the design is correct, many communication blockages can be reduced and proactive strategies developed. One of the greatest potential gains of a positive organization development effort is the unfreezing of certain attitudes that may be retarding efforts at change and proactive strategy formulation. Once these attitudes are unfrozen, it becomes the job of the small business manager to help develop—through visible actions—more positive attitudes. The loss in productivity due to poor human interaction, petty jealousies, role ambiguity, communication mishaps, and an inability to confront difference, is so great that organization development can contribute much to improving the functioning of the small firm's human assets.

Reasons Why Training Efforts Fail

Although significant sums of money are spent on training and development, many programs do not deliver. Training is often viewed as a game divorced from the really "important" things going on. Here are some of the more fundamental reasons for training failures.

Unclear objectives and poor evaluation

Even though management by objectives (MBO) is one of the most widely used developmental approaches, many training efforts have developed few clear and measurable objectives. The training program design is sometimes assumed to be an end in itself, rather than a means to the end. The ultimate test of training effectiveness exists in the real environment, not in the training laboratory or classroom.

It is not good enough to say that the objective of the training session is, for example, to make better supervisors out of the participants. Specific areas of improvement (such as delegation, communication, and discipline) must be highlighted, and specific measurable objectives that are capable of evaluation must be listed and adhered to. Obviously, the evaluation serves to monitor the effectiveness of the training sessions, but more importantly it demonstrates to the participants that the application and implementation of the material is based on current realities. What greater motivator and reinforcer can exist for the participants than the demonstrable, factual evidence of on-the-job improvement?

Overkill

Promising too much, too soon, and too often is responsible for the failure of many training programs. Those in training, who are eager to provide service, often fail to show the line manager (in whose domain the training occurs) that, as in all other organizational activities, good training results stem from hard, dedicated work effort and commitment. Painless solutions to painful problems just do not exist. A frank discussion of the realities of successful training with line managers would do much to clear up the skepticism that many people have about training efforts. It is essential for everyone to understand that training is a slow process, but one that can lead to excellent results if it is performed correctly.

The line manager must be brought into the design of the program and must share in the responsibility for its success. He should not be allowed to delegate the training responsibility to any other person or function. The line manager's commitment to the training effort can only be gained by understanding what training is trying to accomplish. Promising impossible results leads to eventual distrust of the training effort, which in turn leads to a lack of support, thereby contributing to the program's failure.

Incongruence with reward system

Training either involves increasing the skill capabilities of the participants or trying to develop new attitudes and value systems in the participants. If this potential for change is not recognized in the reward system of the organization, there will be little reinforcement to strengthen the training efforts' intended results. New abilities and new attitudes that allow for the assumption of more authority and responsibility must be reflected in the reward and promotion systems.

If there is a lack of congruence between the reward system and the increased employee capability due to training, the participants may well develop the feeling that they are being exploited. Management must take into account the new skills gained. Increased value requires increased recognition, less structure, and more autonomy.

Lack of follow-up

Without adequate follow-up to help the participants apply new concepts to the real work environment, frustration may be the only recognized result of the training effort. A good general rule is to be very skeptical of the possible accomplishments of training efforts unless follow-up sessions are planned. Ideally, this follow-up should be loosely structured and should allow the participants a full opportunity to delve into issues.

Training without follow-up is wasted money. Often it is easier to start piecemeal activities than to develop coordinated, total programs. However, programs without follow-up fail to test the real environment and are therefore unsuccessful. In addition, follow-up provides encouragement and support to the view that training is worth the effort.

The void in career planning

Each position in the organization must have clear-cut criteria for staffing, so that the training program can become a means of combining individual career plans and goals with organizational needs and priorities. Career planning, a process in which individuals choose specific avenues for potential advancement, must be made available to those who are undergoing training. By indicating potential paths for advancement and the role that training performs in providing help along these paths, it can do much to enhance the credibility of training efforts. Career planning also maps out precisely what training must be completed before the assumption of new duties can begin.

Fads, games, and assorted nonsense

Over the past few years, many kinds of experiential exercises have been developed to help make training efforts more effective. Through involvement and participation, various games have added much to the accomplishment of successful training. Instead of listening to theoretical discussion, people learn by doing, although it is essential that the purposes of the games and their relationship to the "real world" be stressed—games for games' sake serve no useful end. Remember, even though the purpose and applications of the games may be obvious to the trainer, they must also be made clear to the participants. Experiential exercises without a tie-in to the work world is not experiential learning.

An example of a widely used game is the bridge exercise in which supervisors bid for and eventually attempt to build a miniature model bridge. Communication patterns, authority relationships, management styles, and delegation patterns—these are just a few of the areas open for discussion after the exercise. Experiential exercises serve a real purpose, but they must be tied in with the daily environment, and the learning that results from them must be coupled with on-the-job application.

Training—Not Just for the New Employee

The one constant in the business world is change, and change requires new skills and abilities. Thus, training should not be limited to the new employee; training is a constant process for employees at all stages of career development and of longevity with the firm. The small business manager is saying in effect that the older employee who is not being trained for new challenges has reached his full potential, since he or she can go no further. Training should be incorporated into the career planning process to allow all employees to develop to their greatest potential and to contribute their maximum.

Many small business managers have a belief that if they train an employee "too much," he or she will leave for new challenges. This belief is often backed by numerous experiences. Of course, the real culprit is not the training but the failure of the organization itself in one of two areas. Either the manager did not understand the purpose of the training and did not change duties and responsibilities accordingly, or else the trainee was incapable of putting the new knowledge to work in the firm. Small business managers frequently remember that "overtrained" employees, who contribute less than their optimum but remain at their jobs, are also a cost. Trained employees may be more difficult to handle because they want to apply new ideas and to improve the place. A small firm that does not "lose" any employees to other organizations may well have employees that nobody else thinks are competent. The challenge for the small business manager is to allow trained employees to stay in the organization, and to contribute their fullest while furthering the organization. (See the Appendix for a guide to gaining better results from management training and development.)

When there are enough people to justify the expense, training efforts can be specifically designed for the small firm. For example, tailored courses in supervisory training can be brought into the firm in several ways. An individual can be sent to a training session with the express purpose of "teaching others" back home, or specific services can be hired. The advantage of this "back home" approach is that it tends to ensure real-life-based discussions, because the group has a similar frame of reference. Yet the cross-fertilization and possibilities of new exposure that are present in mixed groups may be missing.

The small business manager also has to decide who should deliver the training. Outsiders offer both advantages and disadvantages. They are divorced from the organization's political intrigue and thus can give independent advice. Of course, it may be difficult for the outside trainer to become aware of organizational realities and of specific problems regarding implementation. Another concern is the "airport expert," the trainer or consultant who flies in and out of cities on a daily, rotating basis. Many times these experts are not available for adequate follow-up (a vital part of *all* training efforts) and also are not there for the gutsy questions that arise after the initial session.

On the other hand, training that is provided by a regular employee may be suspect, because it often lacks the expertise and insightfulness of more professional approaches. In addition, it is difficult for trainer-employees to wear two hats. The other employees often tend to be skeptical of their presentation and ideas, and they may well be viewed as a "voice" of management. Yet this approach is relatively economical and also provides continuity. Perhaps the best solution is to bring in an outsider. This person can provide continuity, availability, and consistency, can deliver the initial program, and in the process can adequately train and monitor an employee-trainer, who will then take over if the training proves successful.

Who Does the Training?

The small firm usually does not have a formal training department. In most cases, the training and development that the small firm can accomplish with its internal resources is limited and confined to specific skills, such as machine operations, cashier training, and safety training. Other more sophisticated training—such as supervisory and management development and specific staff expertise development—are usually provided by outside resources.

The most common kind of outside resource utilization is to send selected people to various seminars sponsored by schools, trade associations, or consulting firms in the hope that the knowledge they bring back will infuse the organization and help it become more effective. The small business manager should investigate the nature of the outside program thoroughly before investing in it, because the costs are usually substantial (in tuition, travel expenses, board, and time off from normal duties) and the payoff may be questionable. It is naive to think that the training "cannot hurt"; it can. If the person sent by the small firm is exposed to ideas and concepts that are impossible to put into practice in a real work environment, harm will be done, and the individual may become skeptical and critical.

Outside schools and seminars have a lot to offer, but the small business manager must research the need, the service, the content, and the applicability. Many programs promise more than they deliver and are insensitive to the realities of small firms. Perhaps the best way to judge the worth of a program is to discuss it with people who have attended earlier sessions. The small business manager should also level with himself about his own commitment to buy into new ideas, strategies, and approaches so that training will result in improved organization capabilities—not frustration.

9

Know you a man of business who cannot stop when he has finished, who cannot simplify his thoughts, who cannot clarify what he has said? Grieve for this man. He cannot communicate. As a man of business, he is doomed.

ANONYMOUS

creating effective communications

SOMETIMES EFFECTIVE COMMUNICATION is nothing more or less than listening to what other people are saying. Some people feel that the communication process has ceased to function if they are not speaking, and they rarely take the time to hear what the other person or group is saying. Instead, they are concentrating on the next thing *they* are about to say.

Effective communication involves *receiving* messages or signs as well as broadcasting them. Effective communicators sometimes receive no verbal information. A portion of their time is spent reading information they can communicate later. Communication suffers many of the shortcomings of small business: there is very little time for idle chatter; messages are brief and concise, and are clearly shaped by a critical time frame; and people must be able to communicate for understanding—and do it quickly. Figure 2 depicts a model showing the six parts of the communication process. The terms shown on that figure are defined as follows:

Thinking and encoding. Thoughts often take the form of pictures in the human mind. Sometimes these images are vague; at other times the scenes are very detailed. Most of our thoughts stay locked within our minds, but others move out into the world through communication. A thought is converted to a potential communication by an internal process called encoding. Sometimes this process can be difficult to complete—for example, when we wish to say something but we don't quite know how to put it into words. The thought exists, but a gap occurs in the conversion process.

Transmission. The way a communication leaves the sender, a transmission, may be as simple as the wink of an eye, or it could encompass everything necessary to support a world-wide satellite television broadcast. Many forms of transmission are used in small business communication, including memos, reports, telephone con-

Figure 2. Some steps in the communication process.[1]

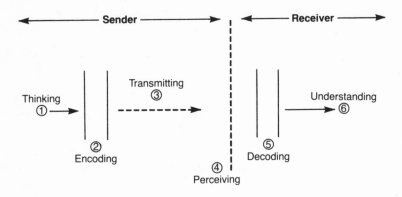

From David R. Hampton, Charles E. Summer, and Ross A. Webber, *Organizational Behavior and the Practice of Management.* Copyright © 1973 by Scott, Foresman & Co. Reprinted with permission.

versations, and handshakes. Each of these forms can transmit communications.

Perception, decoding, understanding. At this point the communications process first relates to the message receiver. Perceptions evolve from the receiver's background, level of understanding, experience, and feelings about both the sender and his or her message. We all have feelings, thoughts, and opinions about the messages we receive. These constitute our individual perceptions. In this way, we screen the messages received, and then "decode" them in order to understand the meaning of the message.

Small organizations need good communications involving a minimum of distortion, ambiguity, and noise. This can be achieved by keeping the messages short, simple, clear, and to the point. Communicate what has to be communicated in a way that promotes clear understanding. If you use this as a guide, you can achieve good communication in a small business.

Some Characteristics of Good Communication

Good communication occurs when the receiver understands the message given by the sender and indicates his understanding through appropriate action. Clarity cannot be achieved merely by virtue of one's position within the small firm. The owner must take individual responsibility to ensure that communications are understood. The same effort to communicate properly is shared by everyone within the organization, using these key characteristics to promote better communications.

Message clarity. Small organization communications can achieve a high degree of clarity when everyone, including the owner, takes the time to send clear messages. Understanding the point of view of message receivers is one step toward clearer communications. Empathy for the other person promotes a warm, receptive feeling for the message. The sender should take the necessary time to determine the reasons for a lack of understanding if it exists, and should take the necessary action to correct it.

For example, feedback from employees may indicate to the owner that his communications are not effective, and corrective action can then be taken. A unique opportunity exists within the small organization for clear communications. Many barriers to clear communication (such as distortion, ambiguity, and tradition) are minimized in small business organizations because of the few people involved.

Physical layout. Another factor that can promote good communication is the physical layout of the organization. A small business can easily be arranged to afford good communications patterns among workers. For example, a receptionist may be situated so that he or she can communicate with walk-in customers and other employees. The relationship between physical layout and employee communication is significant where more than one functional area is handled by a worker. Modern office equipment is designed to be moved as needed. As the organization grows, communication patterns change and physical layout changes can help to maintain proper employee interaction.

Few people are involved. Most small business communication is face to face between individuals. The owner knows all or almost all employees by name. Everyone involved in the business knows special terms and buzz words that make individual communication easier. For example, the owner may need information from a production manager, a salesperson, and a billing clerk. In a large organization, a multiple contact involving different working and supervisory levels would require individual telephone calls and personal coordination. It would be a time-consuming effort that would be handled through the boss's secretary and through various departments. In a small business, however, one or two telephone calls from the owner would be sufficient to resolve the matter. It is easier to communicate when fewer people are involved.

Personal communication. Personal communication has decided advantages over other indirect methods. One advantage is the use of nonverbal signs and signals which sometimes communicate as much as, or more than, spoken messages. Also, the chance of misunderstanding decreases. A big plus in small business communication is the strong rapport that exists among employees. The owner can communicate by means of a brief, personal visit to the parties concerned. He or she can be just as much at ease with the clerk as with the supervisor and salesperson. Or the employees may even be on a first-name basis with the owner.

High level of interest and understanding between parties. Good communication can be fostered through employee interest in the small business. Everyone in the firm understands what the company is all about. Employees tend to become personally involved, and therefore know something about the business—its goals, objectives, and mode of operation. Employee interest in the small company can be reflected in the behavior of the person who is willing to work without normal pay. When the Kentucky Fried Chicken organization was small and struggling, Colonel Sanders had to skimp wherever possible. He paid the office employees in shares of stock rather than dollars. Of course, some years later, the employees were more than repaid through stock appreciation. Some even became millionaires.

Personal sacrifice is a two-way street for employees. They know that it may help them to keep their jobs, and the owner is well aware of their contribution in times of stress. If the company survives and good times come again, the employee will reap his reward. These situations can promote a deep relationship which makes a positive contribution to communication.

Barriers to Effective Communication

One of the most serious barriers in small organizations is the failure of the leader to recognize the need for good communications. The situation is further aggravated where the owner does not admit that communications problems exist. The people in the company take their cues, good or bad, from the person at the top.

Lack of organization. Another barrier to good communication results from poor business organization. This situation is easy to identify. The business operation is carried on in a haphazard way, and things seem to happen more by chance than by direction. An example of this problem is the owner who is consistently absent from the business operation. Sometimes the mere presence of the owner can be a major contributing factor in organizational health. Employees behave differently, feel more secure, and are more polite to customers when the boss is present. A good structural organization setting provides an excellent framework for effective communications. The absence of such a framework can be a serious barrier to communications.

Diverse communications viewpoint. Personal interests of individual employees may differ from those of the owner. When the owner communicates with the employees, he or she should understand that they may perceive these communications in a different manner than was intended.

The sender in this situation may take some additional steps to ensure better communications, such as preconditioning, through employee training; established business communications procedures; follow-up measures to ensure that communications are understood and acted upon properly by employees; and constant procedure improvement through multiple channel use.

The owner must develop a communications awareness program that helps improve all personal message channels within the business. Personal attention to the information needs of all employees will help to overcome the viewpoint barrier and improve *all* communications.

Distractions as a communication barrier. Poor communications may result from situations that are external to the communications process itself. Geographic distance may be a barrier to adequate communication, but this can be corrected by using the proper devices for sending messages. Multiple activities occurring simultaneously interfere with the communications process, because management may send too many messages too quickly. This creates a feeling of frustration among employees about the priority in which communications should be handled. The situation may be easily remedied by timing messages carefully. If carried to extremes, frustration results in most messages being "tuned out" by their intended receivers. Channel variation and proper timing can reduce the problem and eventually correct it. Each communications barrier can be overcome by carefully studying the problem, and by introducing necessary changes to improve the system.

10

motivation:
a practical approach

WHAT IS IT that makes one person eager to begin the job every morning and another hate the thought of even having to get up and go to work? Although there are many different reasons for these divergent outlooks, individual motivation—or the lack of it—lies behind these vastly different approaches to work.

Managers in a small business operation may be highly motivated by the knowledge that their decisions will have a critical effect on the organization every day. In a similar fashion, workers in the small company may realize that their productivity on the job will be directly related to the overall company performance. All employees may be motivated to some extent to do their best job so that they will in fact have a job in the future. Some factors that relate to employee job motivation are discussed in the following sections to help small business owners understand what they can do to encourage their workers.

Traditional Forms of Motivation

Volumes of theoretical material have been written about worker motivation, but the conclusions often lack real practical application. Traditional theory tells us two basic things: most early managers believed that workers were motivated *only* by the need for money, and that motivation was constant over time and varied little from one organization to the next. Business owners and managers know today with some certainty that wages are only one factor (although a very important one) among many that contribute to employee motivation on the job. Status, working conditions, career development, and fringe benefits also serve as effective worker motivators. Small business owners need to offer the best available motivational factors to their employees.

Consider the following situation. A small business had difficulty keeping young female employees, and wage increases did not slow the turnover rate. After much soul-searching about this matter, management realized that the problem was caused by the fact that many of the women were reluctant to leave their young children unattended after school. A new policy was instituted to change some working hours to coincide with the sessions at the local school. As a result, the turnover rate dropped among women who had school-age children. Thus, a simple solution solved a serious problem for the company.

This kind of problem is encountered in one form or another every day. The motivational pattern of the employee is constantly changing, and yesterday's successful motivational tools can readily become today's rusty equipment. What was graciously received by employees in the past (for example, a Christmas turkey or an employee picnic) may be a serious bone of contention for workers today, because motivational factors change.

One small company used to take all of its employees on a one-week paid vacation trip. At first, everyone went as a group. But when the company got larger, some employees resented having to take a trip with the other employees at one specific time. Eventually the trip was discontinued because it provoked so much dissension. This illustrates how management must recognize motivational change and be prepared to provide new solutions to maintain a healthy organizational climate.

The Maslow model of motivation

Among the traditional writers on motivation was Dr. Abraham Maslow, who believed that motivation resulted from an attempt to satisfy individual needs. He conceived of motivation as a motive for action and believed that all of us responded to satisfy certain needs. Maslow indicated an ordering or hierarchy for these needs and formed a five-level pyramid to further explain how people were motivated. Figure 3 shows Maslow's pyramid with the five identified levels of motivational satisfaction to which people aspire.[1]

An important aspect of Maslow's hierarchy, as it is called, is that a person begins with the physical needs at the base of the pyramid and works through each successive level until the individual goals or objectives that have been set are attained. Once the physical needs are satisfied, they no longer motivate the individual. Then, emphasis shifts to the next highest level. Maslow maintained that a satisfied need is no longer a motivator. Hunger is a motivator only as long as the individual is hungry. Once that need is satisfied, higher-level needs provide motivation for individual performance.

In economics, the same concept is illustrated by what is known as the marginal utility concept—that is, the individual derives a great deal of enjoyment or utility from the first big salary increase. Each succeeding raise, however, would provide less utility for the worker, since financial needs would decrease proportionately as wages increased. An extreme example of this concept is when an employee refuses a raise because it would put him or her

[1] Abraham H. Maslow, *Motivation and Personality* (New York: Harper & Row, 1954), pp. 80–91.

Figure 3. Maslow's motivational pyramid.

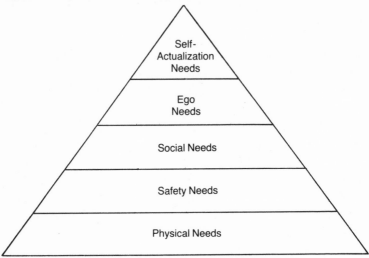

in a higher income-tax bracket. This concept also applies to motivation. More of something is not necessarily good, especially if the individual's needs have been satisfied. And when these needs have been satisfied, the motivational value of the enticement disappears, and management must try other kinds of motivational rewards.

Physical needs. The most basic physical needs include food, clothing, and shelter. Individual workers who are hungry all the time or who cannot buy adequate shelter will not be motivated by any higher-level needs in the pyramid. In such cases, the search for food or shelter becomes the primary means of motivation. The individual is so concerned with these most basic needs that little thought can be given to satisfying any other needs. Once physical needs have been reasonably satisfied, a person can focus on making sure that the environment is safe and secure enough to allow him or her to enjoy continued satisfaction of physical needs.

Safety needs. A person's safety needs are satisfied when management provides both physical safety on the job and a degree of emotional safety and security *in* the job by means of employment stability and proper training. Safety plays such an important part in work today that unsafe conditions can cause entire operations to be shut down. This to a large extent has been removed from the decision-making framework of the small business person and is now in the province of the government. Yet the *emotional* safety of employees is still an important consideration for the small business person. Employees want to understand the rules of the game, to have a sense of what is expected of them, and to know that as long as they do follow those rules they will be secure in their positions.

Social needs. Once the physical and safety needs have been satisfied, people's needs turn toward a less tangible kind of satisfaction. People are basically gregarious animals. They like to gather in groups and seek the approval of the groups to which they belong. Social needs are quite important on the job. Organizations make it essential for one to associate with other people on the job. Yet, many small businesses have few formal opportunities for interaction among employees on anything outside work-related issues.

However, a lack of social contact on the job is not necessarily bad. A small business manager can provide other means to help employees satisfy their social needs. Management can encourage employees to get together during leisure hours through company-sponsored picnics or outings. Some organizations sponsor sports teams for employees. Baseball, basketball, bowling, and golf are all group activities that help meet employee social needs. These activities are important because they provide opportunities for employee motivation through the satisfaction of social needs.

Ego needs. Ego satisfaction is derived by personal achievement on the job, through the job, and about the job. Many times we are our own worst critics, especially if what we do satisfies other people but does not meet our own performance standards. Many opportunities exist in the small business for satisfying ego needs—if certain conditions are present. These conditions include the motivation of the individual who has the desire to perform well at a given job. True ego satisfaction demands an organization structure in which the employee can grow and progress through individual effort toward job growth and career development.

The small business structure can foster satisfaction of ego needs through individual achievement much quicker than can large, monolithic companies where "each must wait his turn." Small businesses can also provide ego satisfaction through worker visibility to top management. A job well done comes to management's attention almost immediately. Management can provide additional opportunities for good employees and thereby reinforce their ego feelings. Successful mastery of present challenges leads to stronger motivation through ego satisfaction.

Self-actualization needs. Self-actualization refers to "doing one's own thing." In a job situation, the concept of self-actualization means that the employee would rather do this particular job than almost any other job that is available. If an employee is motivated to this degree, the organization provides the kind of environment in which an individual finds a challenge at the highest possible level.

Many small business organizations provide opportunities for self-actualization which are not found in larger companies. For instance, smaller companies require individuals to accept greater responsibility, even at lower levels in the hierarchy. Also, the quality of individual decisions must be high, since action will probably be taken on many of them quickly. Small organizations have little or no organizational "fat," and decisions cannot languish or get lost in a maze; every decision counts. For the alert employee who is willing to be decisive and to accept more duties, there is the possibility of increased visibility and recognition.

The Herzberg model of motivation

Frederick Herzberg has also made a major contribution to the field of motivation. He classifies most job determinants, including money, as "hygiene factors"—that is, they are a necessary part of the job itself, but they make no significant contribution to individual motivation. Herzberg's model of motivation differs from Maslow's, but certain key factors are similar. According to Herzberg, recognition, achievement, responsibility, and advancement are really key contributors to motivation, and their presence will help motivate employees. Notice that money is *not* a factor in Herzberg's model. This is a significant contribution to motivation theory. It is also a clear message to small business owners: provide opportunities for recognition and achievement and you will really be able to motivate people. It is a matter of understanding employee needs through whatever means are available to the organization. The best form of motivation depends on the employee and the particular situation. There is no one best answer.

One of the most important factors in determining the possible success of managers in small firms is understanding their motive patterns. A motive pattern consists of the things that make a manager tick. It is in essence a rationale for explaining what needs are satisfied by certain types of behavior.

Research shows that motivation patterns center on three basic dimensions: achievement, power, and affiliation. Achievement is the need to excel, to accomplish, and to complete. Power motivation exists when one wants to influence and control others. Affiliation motivation is manifested by a desire to befriend others and to become involved with them. In the small firm, successful entrepreneurs usually have high achievement needs, as opposed to the high power needs of the top executives in the larger firm. The entrepreneur wants to achieve excellence and is constantly searching for challenging fields that demand excellence. The typical large business manager may also have achievement objectives, but he or she has a greater need to control and influence others and tends to be prone to empire-building. (In the Appendix is a test that will give you insight into your own motivation patterns—and, hence, other people's as well.)

Motivation that the Small Business Can Offer Employees

Sometimes, people tend to associate the concept of "big" with "best." In terms of worker motivation, that association may be misleading. Large organizations can sometimes "lose" people. No one steals them, and the individuals don't disappear; they just become lost in the organizational labyrinth. Small businesses and organizations seldom have this problem: there are few hiding places, and anyone who is gone for even a short time is missed by the others. Here are some features of small businesses which make them attractive to people who want to excel and which are thus excellent motivators.

A chance to make meaningful decisions. In most small organizations the interested employee has ample opportunity to make decisions that have a direct impact on the business organization—decisions that are important in their direct effect on the well-being of the company are made comparatively far down the organizational structure. Therefore, the employee who is willing to contribute his time and talents to the company will find that his word and opinions do have weight in the decision-making process. This kind of contribution can result in rapid advancement, along with commensurate monetary and other benefits for the striving individual.

Possibility of assuming the entire business operation. In small companies, employees may still start at the bottom of the ladder and eventually work their way right up to the top job. This situation exists in every company, but the odds of starting in the mailroom at General Motors or Xerox and working your way up through the ranks to become the president of the company are so slim that by comparison a single ticket on the Irish Sweepstakes would be a sure winner. But the odds of the right person's starting at the bottom of a small organization and working up to the top are good. And even in family-owned businesses, sometimes the children of the owner want nothing to do with the business when they grow up. Under these circumstances, an opportunity exists for the outside employee to purchase the business outright.

Career path development for the new employee. Everyone working today is interested in career path development. Simply stated, this means that the individual employee builds up and maintains expectations with regard to his or her job progression. The path to the top of a small company is shorter than any similar path in a medium-size or large organization. These expectations often mesh with an organization's future manpower needs. There can be less uncertainty of the future in the small firm, depending on the owner's actions. The key individual may personally ensure employee career development or even future ownership agreements involving the employee. This word of concern, hope, expectation, and promise is often a unique motivator for the employee in the small firm.

Increased capability expectation. Part of the career path development process is closely allied with company expectations about the job. It is one thing to write job specifications, but it is something else to be able to provide constant development in job content. Job qualifications change, and the requirements to fill those positions change; therefore, employees in the small company must be encouraged to constantly upgrade their skills so that their value to the organization will grow and deepen as additional duties are assumed. Small firms pride themselves on loyalty and low turnover, and increased skills are expected of present employees.

Many years ago, it may have been enough to have a job and come to work. Today, this is not true. People want to know how their jobs are going to fit into the organizational framework and how their performance in these jobs will affect the overall performance of the company. Good managers respect the individual right to know, and they do what they can to keep workers informed.

Consideration for individual abilities. The small business manager realizes that employees need consideration for their individual characteristics and capabilities as well as for their contribution on the job. For example, the small organization offers much more room for an individual to move completely out of one operational area of the business and into another. In so doing, the employees may develop more talent than either they or the organization suspected that they had.

Organizational rewards must be available to the employee who is willing to follow this strategy instead of the normal development or the "managed" progression followed by larger companies. As the small business develops, there will probably be ample financial growth and emotional rewards to satisfy the energetic employee who has met the organization's test. Management knows that employees will constantly evaluate their own progress in the company.

Long-term relationship. The longer an employee remains in a small organization, the more valuable that employee should become. If this does not happen, it means that the small business manager has failed to provide an environment conducive to development. A committed employee thinks, feels, and acts appreciatively toward the employer. This may be expressed through extra actions and personal sacrifices that the employee is willing to make as part of the job. In the early stages of a company's development, management tends to appreciate these sacrifices; yet something happens as the organization matures and as former sacrifices tend to become present expectations. What is needed is a constant awareness or recognition of employees who are willing to "go the extra mile" or spend the extra time to see that their jobs are done.

Small business managers can take a hint from their counterparts in the big organization and provide night school opportunities, extra vacation wages, or a company-sponsored trip if that is appropriate; however, the small business manager does not have to stop here. To a conscientious, long-term employee, many individual opportunities are open in small organizations that large companies cannot provide. In a sense, the small company can provide individually tailored opportunities for career advancement within the framework of the organization. The small business manager is not encumbered by too many rules, policies, and traditions in the area of individual employee rewards. Each employee can be treated in a special way. No blanket labor contract need apply to all.

Conclusion

Basically, the question of motivation begins when the first employee is hired, and it continues throughout the life of the organization. (Notice that no assumption has been made that a small organization always grows into a large organization, as an acorn grows into a mighty oak. Small organizations can be successful and still survive while remaining small.) The emphasis here has been on the survival of the organization and the importance of motivation in selecting good employees. Other important factors are training employees to accept additional responsibilities, encouraging individual development, and providing employees with some tangible planned career path development program that will enable the organization to keep the necessary people. These, then, are some important aspects of motivation in small business organizations, and in many ways they offer much more to employees than larger companies can.

11

Thou are not able to perform it alone . . .
EXODUS XVIII

delegating for results

MANAGEMENT ASSISTANCE for the small business manager comes in almost every conceivable size, shape, and functional area (such as insurance, accounting, finance, marketing, legal, and production). Generally, the small business manager will not, and probably cannot, be as competent in these domains as specialized outside resource people would be. Thus, the policies affecting the operations of the small business will to a large degree be influenced by outside "experts" in their particular fields of knowledge. Outsiders can, of course, only advise the independent business person, but in today's complex business environment, sound advice is often closely related to actual decision-making policy.

The manager of the small business should understand that outside resource people do not have the degree of commitment and feeling for the business that the owner and the work team have. Some consultants make all kinds of complex recommendations for the organization yet never stay around long enough to see that these recommendations are implemented properly.

Outside assistance of any kind, regardless of its quality and degree, cannot and must not substitute for the authority and dedication of the small business manager. In a very real sense the small business manager is like the head of a family, and his decisions, which are made as a result of the judicious use of wisdom and experience, are the major determinants of the success or failure of the family relationship. There may be a wide spectrum of outside help to "assist" the head of the family; however, any abdication of responsibility by the head of the family can be disastrous. This is also true for the small business manager: taking an outsider's advice is worlds apart from *abdication* by the manager to some outside force. The small business manager has and must retain the ultimate decision-making authority. The buck stops at his desk.

The one function that the small business person must always perform is the basic management duty of achieving effective human relationships that lay the groundwork for attaining organizational objectives. No matter what the specific nature of the industry may be, all managers are basically in the people business, and the small business manager is in the people business more than other managers. With fewer people at his disposal, the small business manager must use each one effectively. There is no room for poor performers; the scope of the business is too small to carry an extra burden.

In a small firm, each employee is vital. One disgruntled employee can sabotage and destroy the work efforts of all. Effective human relationships are the basis for successful managerial action, and all the outside management assistance in the world cannot make the organization succeed if its human development capabilities are not up to par. The kind of relationship that exists between the small businessman and his subordinates is not determined by outside expertise; it is determined by the businessman's management philosophy. A real source of internal expertise is always available to the small businessman—available, that is, if he takes the time to train and develop it.

Delegation Is Not New

Perhaps the most difficult thing for the small businessman to develop is a management philosophy that recognizes the vital need for delegating responsibilities. This recognition must then be followed by an action plan for implementation.

In a small firm, each decision is critical. There is little room for error and few resources to fall back on to absorb mistakes. In addition, the owner of the small firm has at one time or another probably done just about every job in the organization, so he is familiar with many more aspects of the firm than the typical manager in the larger organization. For this reason there is often a tendency for a small businessman to want to continue doing everything. But as the business grows, new areas must occupy the entrepreneur's interest and of course take up his time. The need for delegation becomes obvious—delegation is essential if the firm is to continue to succeed.

In the larger firm that has more formal and less personal job descriptions, delegation is merely assigning to a person the necessary authority (the right to perform) along with the appropriate responsibility (the obligation to perform). In the smaller firm, the person doing the delegating and giving up part of his authority is often the founder. Thus, it is not merely a question of the right wording on a job description; it is personal. When the small business person delegates, he gives up part of himself. It is his firm, his capital, and his ideas, and he rightly believes that if it weren't for him the company wouldn't be successful. So why should he delegate? The answer is simple: he must delegate to ensure that the organization can meet new challenges by enhancing its effectiveness and developing its human resources, which are its most important asset.

One of the earliest recorded examples of one person's advising another to delegate responsibility appears in the Bible (Exodus XVIII), where Moses' father-in-law, Jethro, says to Moses:

> What is this thing that thou doest to the people: Why sittest thou thyself alone, and all the people stand about thee from morning until evening? . . .

To this Moses replies:

> Because the people come unto me to inquire of God . . .

Jethro then clearly points out the need to delegate:

> The thing that thou doest is not good. Thou will surely wear away, both thou, and this people that is with thee; thou are not able to perform it alone . . . Moreover thou shalt provide out of all the people able men, such as fear God, men of truth, hating unjust gain; and place such over them. To be rulers of thousands, rulers of hundreds, rulers of fifties, and rulers of tens. And let them judge the people at all seasons; and it shall be very great matter they shall bring unto thee, but every small matter they shall judge themselves; so shall they make it easier for thee and bear thy burden with thee.

The manager must therefore choose good people according to specified criteria, and assign them subordinate responsibilities. The criteria he uses to select these people must be related to the nature of the job to be accomplished. Honesty, integrity, follow-up, and determination are essential criteria, whereas the amount of specific technical knowledge required—finance, marketing, and accounting—depends on the situation. All in all, the small business manager must inventory the available skills and traits with each opportunity. The delegation process has the hidden benefit of demanding that the owner-manager become more aware of employees' individual strengths and weaknesses and use these as a basis for work assignment.

The Reasons People Resist Delegating Responsibilities

But if delegation has so much to offer, why don't more managers use it to their advantage? Or is the advice given to Moses by Jethro no longer applicable? The answer is that effective delegation takes time to perfect and it is difficult to carry out. Patience is needed, and in an action environment this can be frustrating. The benefits of delegation do not come about without an investment. Some managers simply feel that their subordinates cannot be trusted with additional, meaningful responsibility. But this state of affairs gives some insight not only into the employee, but also into the manager who would hire people with such limited ability. Failure to delegate must ultimately be related to the boss's lack of trust—either in his own ability to train people or in the ability of his subordinates to perform. Common rationalizations that disguise lack of trust of employees often include these:

"I can do it better myself."

"She'll take care of the details, but will miss the main point."

"I'm not sure of his judgment in a pinch."

"He's too young to command the respect of the other people."

"She's much too emotional to handle crises."

"I like to keep busy."

"My subordinates lack experience."

"My people won't accept responsibility."

"I can't afford mistakes."

All of these statements tell us more about the small business person than about the employees. They hint of fear, lack of trust, and mediocre job performance standards, as well as poor hiring policies. Sometimes this negative outlook leads to self-fulfilling prophecies: if the small business manager really believes that delegation will not work, he will consciously and unconsciously act in a manner that will allow his suspicions to be confirmed.

One fear that should be noted is the psychological fear of not being needed or, at the very least, of being less valuable to the organization. This is indeed a real fear that is often the largest barrier to delegation. We all take our abilities for granted and assume that what we do requires no really special talent. But to the outsider, an individual's specific job is really quite complex and demands much skill, but in performing the duty the individual has done the job so well for so long a time that the job seems routine, as if anybody could do it. But good managers will always be needed by the firm, and delegating responsibilities is a way of making the highest contribution to the organization, since it will mean a division of tasks commensurate with everybody's abilities. Delegation is needed by the boss to allow more effective use of his abilities; by the subordinate to allow for development and growth; and by the firm to allow for effective policy formulation and implementation.

Our experience has convinced us that many small business people want to delegate various functions, but simply don't know how. With this in mind, the following guides may be useful.

Guides to Delegation

In the rest of this chapter, practical guidelines are offered to the small business manager to help integrate the concept of delegation into his or her management technique. This list is by no means exhaustive, but the items can serve as an initial guide for small business managers who may want to sharpen their delegating skills.

Delegation is not abdication

When someone delegates responsibility and authority to another, he does not remove himself totally from the picture. Indeed, the small business manager must keep in close contact with the person to whom the specific duty is delegated. If the process is to be successful, delegation demands the utmost in teamwork and in clear, open, and supportive communication. The manager who delegates by abdication is doomed to poor results. Indeed, in its initial stages, delegation may require more communication and even more paperwork to assure success. But this investment should pay dividends and will in the long run lessen the superior's time commitment to routine duties.

Delegation is not dumping

All jobs have their pleasant and unpleasant sides, and the small businessman will often use delegation as a way of ridding himself of the unpleasant aspects of a job. Of course, employees perceive the misuse of delegation and sometimes develop an attitude that is reflected in their not wanting to assume additional responsibilities. The solution is to delegate both the good and bad aspects of work assignments. Don't be the driver and always expect the subordinate to fix the flat tire; let him or her enjoy the ride, too! Be honest with yourself about the real purpose of the employee's delegated assignment: is it to increase employee skills or to allow you a chance to avoid an unpleasant task?

Delegate the whole activity

There is a great temptation on the part of many managers to delegate only those tasks or parts of tasks which are of minimal importance. It is characterized by the feeling of always "pulling back" or never really giving the subordinate free reign to do the job. The small business manager must be willing to let the subordinates make their own mistakes. That is how learning occurs for most of us, and there seem to be no real shortcuts to this process. Effective delegation allows mistakes to be made in a guided, controlled, low-risk environment. It allows learning and growth in abilities to take place simultaneously.

No matter how small the activity may be—from stocking a section of a retail market to maintaining a machine—delegate the responsibility for all of it. Allow employees to be put in charge of one entire section of shelf space or of a complete part of the machine. It is easier for employees to get a sense of positive accomplishment if they feel that they have completed an entire task, and this can be an excellent means of reinforcement. For true pride of achievement to exist and grow, meaningful delegation must incorporate meaningful work accomplishment.

Appraise immediately after completion of the task

Rapid feedback is vital if the employee is to use the delegation process as a learning experience. The more rapid the feedback, the greater the chance that the delegation process and its results will be evaluated on an objective basis. The longer the lag between performance and appraisal, the more likely it will be that the actual performance will be forgotten. If appraisal is to have the basic results intended—guidance, improvement, training, and development—appraisal feedback must be closely related in time to actual performance. The longer the time span between performance and appraisal, the hazier the facts will become to both the small business manager and the employee who performed the delegated duty. Appraise immediately after performance—nothing can be gained by waiting.

Delegate by objectives

One of the problems most often encountered by small business people is their tendency to confuse activities with results. Results are the objectives we wish to achieve; activities are the specific methods and actions for reaching the objectives.

Too often, small business managers delegate by activities and not by results. Effective control through monitoring, feedback, and training should ensure that the expected results are achieved, but excessive emphasis on detail tends to discourage initiative on the part of the employee. Don't tell the employee how to hold the putter; just tell him to get the ball in the hole. How he holds the club may be different from the way you would hold it, but if the ball gets in the hole, then the objective will have been reached. Provide guidance but not rigid rules. Concentrate on the results, the actual attainment of objectives—not the individual methods of getting there.

Delegate by stages

The advice Jethro gave Moses is perfectly valid today: delegated duties must be assigned to those who measure up to well-defined criteria. In a small firm, these criteria will be determined by the owner. Yet any chosen criterion—honesty, perseverance, dedication, or the ability to see a job through—takes time to measure and observe. The best way to evaluate employees' abilities to perform up to specific criteria and standards is to note their progress over a period of time. During this time period, delegated activities should increase in size and scope. In this way, past performance can be observed and monitored, guidance offered, and the employee made more capable of taking on increased responsibility.

Dealing with mistakes

Since delegation is a training process, mistakes are bound to occur. The question is not if mistakes will happen, but how to deal with the mistakes that do take place. There are basically three options:

1. Overlook the mistake by saying, "Well, we all have bad days."
2. Treat the mistake harshly and severely discipline the offenders.
3. Deal with the mistake as the symptom, and in the hope of correcting it, try to find out what caused it.

Obviously, the third choice is the most productive. It takes time, but it recognizes the possibility that the boss may be wrong, too. An atmosphere must be created in which the boss is willing to hear about his or her mistakes, so that they can be corrected. Mistakes will occur, whether or not the employees tell the boss about

them. Great amounts of creativity and effort often go into conceal-
ing mistakes rather than rectifying them.

An old story illustrates this point very well. An individual was
to be promoted to chairman of the board on July 1, and on June 30,
a dinner was held in his honor. At this dinner the master of ceremonies introduced the new chairman and noted that this day was
probably the most notable day in his life. When the guest of honor
took the microphone and thanked the M.C. for the introduction
and the company for the dinner, he diplomatically corrected the
M.C. by stating that the *next* day, July 1, would be the most notable
since it was then that he would assume the duties of chairman. To
this the master of ceremonies replied: "No, I wasn't mistaken.
Today is the most notable day, because it's the last day you'll hear
the truth from anybody around here."

Mistakes can be dealt with out of strength or covered up out of
weakness, depending on the particular small business manager.
Delegation should be a growing and learning process. Mistakes will
occur, but they can be limited and new skills, talents, and capabilities can be developed as a result.

What to Delegate

As a general rule, delegation should be practiced when someone
within the organization can do a job better than the small business
manager, instead of the manager, at less expense, with better timing, and in a way that contributes to more training and development than if the small business manager had performed it himself.

The biggest reason for failure in small businesses that at one
time were successful is the inability of management to provide succession through continuity. Delegation is a safeguard against this
potential shortcoming. It is the manager's best investment in his
employees, his business, and himself. Delegation is not easy—it
takes time, commitment, understanding, and constant review to

succeed. Delegation means taking risks, but failure to delegate can be costly. First of all, it can result in a lack of managerial development and training of employees, which will ultimately have disastrous effects on the firm. Another consequence may be the inability of the owner-manager-entrepreneur to use his talents to the fullest, since he is so involved in small things that drain his energy, because no one else is capable of stepping in and doing them.

All functions in a business can be subjected to the delegation process, although traditionally this has happened the least with the financial function. For many good reasons the small business manager frowns on disclosing financial data. We remember a consulting project we once undertook for a small retail firm that was plagued (according to the owner) by employee indifference, complacency, and lack of concern. The greatest problem noted was the inability of the store managers to think of themselves as part of management. The store managers were responsible for such things as payroll, manpower, schedules, and volume. Yet the owner refused to let them know what the overall profit of their stores was, because he felt that he would be disclosing too much. Perhaps this was true, but the fact remained that it was almost impossible for the managers to really do their jobs without this data. It may well be worthwhile to retain certain data privately and keep certain operations centralized; just make sure that the benefits of this approach exceed the cost.

Effective delegation demands that the small business manager develop the ability to direct. He must think ahead and visualize the work situation; formulate objectives and general plans of action; and communicate these plans to his subordinates. Rather than operate on a crisis-by-crisis approach, the manager who uses delegation as part of his management philosophy gains at least as much as the subordinate who assumes new duties: both develop expanded skill and capabilities by taking a more planned approach to managerial action. (There is a series of tests in the Appendix to help you evaluate and improve your own ability to delegate responsibility.)

Delegation provides a mechanism by which each individual develops his or her own management capability. It helps to maintain people's enthusiasm about the organization and prevents employees from quitting while on the job. The payoff from delegation is that the work gets done faster, easier, and at less cost. Delegation is not merely the nice thing to do; it is the right way to manage. In his book *Robert Browning*, G. K. Chesterton described the consequences that occur when people in power fail to delegate responsibility properly:

> It is when men begin to grow desperate in their love for the people, when they are overwhelmed with the difficulties and blunders of humanity, that they fall back upon a wild desire to manage everything themselves. . . . This belief that all would go right if we could only get the strings into our own hands is a fallacy almost without exception, but nobody can justly say that it is not public-spirited. The sin and sorrow of despotism is not that it does not love men, but that it loves them too much and trusts them too little. . . . When a man begins to think that the grass will not grow at night unless he lies awake to watch it, he generally ends either in an asylum or on the throne of an emperor.

12

Life always gets harder toward the summit—
the cold increases, responsibility increases.

setting objectives
and assigning responsibilities

PEOPLE IN SMALL BUSINESS must plan many aspects of their business operation to be certain that things are being carried out properly. Part of the planning process involves setting objectives at various stages in the business's development. Setting objectives and planning are both basic to organizational effectiveness, and large organizations follow very definite procedures in this area. Owners of small business operations have to incorporate objective setting into their conscious planning efforts, since there is less formal structure than in large firms.

The owners of small organizations often seem to drift along from one day to the next without any conscious planning effort. This is not good for the company, and it does not help the owner carry out his personal long-term projects. Therefore, the small business owner will best serve his personnel and company needs by setting objectives as part of an overall planning process. Fulfilling the objectives must become the responsibility of some other individual within the small business. The owner's responsibility should be to ensure that the objectives have been met rather than to accomplish them himself.

The Objective-Setting Process

The first step is to determine what constitutes an objective for the organization. Each objective also relates to a projected time span. Some objectives are short-term, and these differ significantly from objectives that have a long-range impact on company operations. Some owners know intuitively what should be done, but they don't commit their plans to writing. This could be a dangerous situation if the owner should die or become incapacitated. Among the stated objectives, management must determine its priorities. This is necessary to keep all objectives in their proper perspective. Management works with dual agendas for objectives—those that affect the current operation and those that affect the future. Both sets of objectives can and should be developed at the same time.

In small business, many obvious deficiencies go uncorrected at first because all resources must be used to support current operations. For example, an ice cream store sells bulk flavors by weight, but its owner had inherited two ancient balance scales which, because they were not accurate, caused free ounces of ice cream to be given to customers. The problem was solved by replacing the old scales with one digital, solid-state scale that weighs accurately to .01 ounce. Customers gladly pay for the extra one or two ounces, and the businessman no longer loses money. No one doubts the importance of that problem, and the business obviously lost money while the problem existed. In the first days of operation, however, there were several other matters that were significantly more important than replacing the old scales, which was initially conceived of as a long-range problem rather than one that required immediate attention. It was of a lower priority, and therefore had to wait its turn until more important matters had been settled. But it did remain an objective, and eventually it was solved.

Once an objective has been defined, some step toward reaching it should be made. At that point the objective must become the responsibility of management. This second step, implementation, presents difficulties for some small business owners, who have a hard time coming to grips with setting priorities. Objectives are spelled out in plans, and these plans need to be written so that others can understand them. This procedure is vital if the owner works alone, and in that case he or she should discuss the plans with a lawyer and accountant so that if something should happen to the owner, someone else will be able to implement the plans. Proper planning enhances profitable business operations by providing a marked path for controlled growth and development.

Objectives should have proper timing

Sometimes a small organization does not grow. This kind of unplanned stagnation can cause serious difficulties for the business, and it may indicate major problem areas. The owner must examine the reasons for the lack of growth. But paradoxically, a more serious problem can occur when the small organization develops and grows without a plan. Growth without planning can lead to disaster.

The musician needs a score to learn his part. The architect needs a blueprint to build a structure. The small business needs a plan for it to grow. For example, if thorough plans are not made, new employees may be hired without the benefit of training. A growing organization is extremely vulnerable to the disruption caused by improperly hired and inadequately trained employees.

The proper timing of objectives can help prevent unchecked growth of small businesses. As established objectives are met, the company continues to grow. Objectives are reexamined periodically to determine if former priorities are still valid. For example, at the time the plan is developed, it may seem logical to accomplish objectives three and four before completing objectives five and six. But as time goes on, it may become evident that objectives five and six must be accomplished before the others. Thus, the original plan becomes the basis for periodic objective review so that if the original plan were still valid, objectives five and six would be deferred until objectives three and four had been completed; but if the situation changes, the plan can be changed, too, although the concepts behind the original plan should remain the basis for planning.

Management must insist that the plan be followed now to prevent trouble in the future. This may be an unpopular position—outsiders may feel that management is not allowing the company to grow, and those responsible for objectives five and six may feel that their operation is being deliberately held back while other areas are being pushed forward. These concerns are very real. But managers' discontent can be minimized if they are persuaded that these decisions are in the long-run interests of the organization rather than of any individual group.

Present objectives relate to past and future actions

Goal- or objective-setting relates to the future, as present objectives relate to the past. This relationship helps maintain continuity within the business. Past accomplishments and future plans are vital to present activities—not to encourage tradition, but to demonstrate direction and purpose within the company. People tend to feel comfortable when they can see that what is happening today relates to some past plan and that present accomplishments can represent objectives for future development.

Employees like to feel that their work is a visible contribution to the big picture. Feelings of security result from working in a company that has arrived at its present position through some design and is looking toward the future through planned activities. Organizational continuity promotes stability within both management and employee groups.

Someone must be accountable

At meetings, there will often be discussions about matters affecting the organization, and objectives will be set with the consent and approval of the group participants. But if nothing further is done, the written objectives will not be worth the cost of the paper on which they are printed. Many small businesses make the mistake of planning only on paper, and that is where it stays—on paper. Some people will find this situation appealing, because they can participate in the planning process without any responsibilities: no single individual is responsible, and collectively the group cannot be held responsible, either. If the objective is accomplished, so much the better; if it fails, no one is really to blame.

Let us return to this original meeting where an objective is approved, but let's change the scenario a bit. The group agrees, and now it is time to take the final step toward implementation. The chairperson, or the members of the group, assign that responsibility to some individual who may or may not be present at the meeting. Nevertheless, the objective is the responsibility of someone in management—a significant difference from the previous group's anonymous agreement to participate. Now, someone is accountable and must produce the desired results. Failure to do so will invoke sanctions by the group. There is no substitute for getting things done through individuals who are accountable rather than through groups.

Objective implementation: the final test

Organizations move from objective to objective along the path to completion of the plan, but the final point is never reached. The implementation of individual objectives is the only way in which the company can make progress. But implementation of objectives takes patience. Each group has a different perspective on the company's objectives, and the owner must realize that to some extent he has to "sell" his team on the ideas. Employees also like to understand why changes are being made. They want to know how the changes are going to affect their jobs and how they must adjust their work routine to accommodate the changes.

Let's look at two cases of how a certain objective was implemented. Both examples began the same way. A small company decided to implement a small time-sharing computer in its operation. In the planning stages, the objective was handled by the owner of the business who had a very strong feeling for the concept. A feasibility study indicated that a time-sharing computer system would be appropriate. Several months elapsed between the decision to go ahead with the project and the installation of equipment. During that time, the owner kept a close watch on the computer plan idea. The organization continued to expand, and two additional managers were also hired during this time.

In the first case, the computer project was inherited by a mature manager. He had just been hired from a rather conservative company in a field that was not related to that of the small business. This manager had not been exposed to a working computer environment, and he had no strong feelings about what this computer could accomplish. The project received a high priority on the new manager's things-to-do list, partly because it was the boss's pet project, although it was not of compelling interest to this manager. During hardware installation, the manager went through the motions and tried to learn just enough to avoid any criticism by his boss.

The computer project suffered, and eventually died a slow death because the person responsible had not made a personal commitment to the idea. The boss became involved with other questions and did not take time to monitor the progress of the project. He sometimes wondered why the time-sharing system did not seem to be moving along, but he had other responsibilities to occupy his time. So in this example, the objective was implemented, but the right person had not been found to monitor the project. Given those unhealthy conditions, it did not take long for the project to die. Everything went according to plan except the final stage, so the project was a failure.

In the second case, the manager in charge of the project had had prior experience with time-sharing computer systems during his college training. He had also worked with computers in his previous job. In this case, the project also received a high priority, but for different reasons than in the first example: the manager believed in the things that could be accomplished through time sharing, and he contributed several suggestions of his own design which improved the original plan. The installation process went very well because considerable preparatory work and planning had been done. All members of management, including the owner, had been sent to a course offered by the hardware manufacturer. The purpose of the course was to indoctrinate key people about the best use of the computer for their business.

Once operations began, there was little difficulty in maintaining the initial enthusiasm for the computer. Positive results occurred during the first six months' operation. These results were possible because the concept of computer usage had been developed properly in the organization over a long period of time, and because management felt comfortable with the computer system.

The two examples began in the same way, had the same planning, and the same push by the bosses in the early stages, but the endings were quite different. The second example was successful because the right person had been put in charge of the maintenance stage after implementation, and this manager's impact was felt for some time. He was there when he was needed during the early growth stage, and proper follow-through meant success for an important segment of the company operation.

Objectives need monitoring
After implementation, objectives need to be monitored constantly. In the first example, the related activities would have received less emphasis as it became clear to the people responsible

that the main objective was not going to receive the enthusiastic support of top management. Usually, peripheral projects will drop away long before the main objective is abandoned. Perceptive managers realize what is going on, and they will cease nonproductive efforts as soon as possible, because they don't want to be associated with a losing plan. When a plan is perceived to be weak, people will rush to drop it rather than help make it operational. Managers keep pushing those things that are of interest to their bosses. If that interest wanes or disappears, the project and its related activities will be finished.

Objectives are small business owners' responsibility

Small business owners provide planning impetus, constant guidance, and supervision of implementation, as well as a continuing interest in maintaining objectives. The owner has the primary decision-making role in the small company. No board of directors takes up the slack, and no stockholders will insist that certain things be done. The number of employees is not large enough to effect change. Other instances could be cited, but everything still comes back to the starting point: the small business owner can make things happen in the small company—for better or for worse.

The small business owner thus sets the objectives for the company, plans for their success from inception to implementation, and ensures their proper maintenance by selecting the right manager for the job. This is a big responsibility, but objectives need to be the starting point of small business management thought and action.

Planning Ahead and Developing Strategies

Small business management is a multifaceted activity. By this time, you should be asking the questions: "How do I develop strategies to handle the many needs and challenges described so far? What can I do to build a winning team of managers and employees?" This book has attempted to answer these questions. But right now, just stop and think about what you have to do in order to better operate your own small business.

Planning for employees

You know that you are going to plan for your future. What about your employees? Where will they come from? How will you recruit them? How will you reward them? How will you discipline them? How will you communicate with them? How will you train and develop them? What kind of orientation will you provide? What kind of career development pattern are you prepared to offer them? This is most important, because they need to have a career plan through their retirement, just as you do. Think about it: what can you do to help them plan right from the beginning? How can you keep control and at the same time allow for their individual growth?

Your role in the business

Another thing you have to consider is how much the business needs you—that's right, *you*. Employees can't do it all; your presence is necessary. Make a commitment now to spend time in the business. The business must be a major part of your life. Your employees will appreciate you more and will be more effective when you are available to them, because they will be able to get answers to their questions. It's your business, so plan to be there most of the time, and especially when things get hectic—that's when everyone needs you the most.

Plan to meet and greet customers, if your business requires it. If customers contact you by telephone, be sure you're there to answer their calls. This is important, because everyone likes personal attention. Your customers will be happy to see you because they like the attention and personal touch that you provide, and people like to tell their friends that they know the owner personally. It doesn't cost you anything but your time to provide personal service, and the business is bound to grow better and faster when you are there.

What do you know and what can you do?

Another question that you need to consider is, what do you *know* about the business? You can be the smartest person in the world, but if you don't know much about your business and what it does, you will be in for a rough time. Remember, the less you know, the more you will have to rely on employees. But even the most knowledgeable and faithful employees depend on the boss for support. It gives them confidence to know that they can come to you with a knotty problem and that you can help them find the answer. Of course, as the business grows you will need to develop new skills and abilities to be effective in your changing role.

Nobody knows all there is to know about a business when it starts, but you can make plans to attend classes, read books, get individual help, or whatever you need to help you get to know the business better. It's best to learn while the business is new and to continue to learn, because people won't expect as much of you in the beginning as they will after the operation matures. You can profit from early mistakes and build a better operation.

Planning for success and for the future

Businesses often fail for a reason their originators failed to consider: the lack of a good, well-thought-out strategy. A final strategy generally concerns your plans for the business in the future. If you are as successful in reality as you are in theory at the beginning, it means that your business—and you—have done something right.

Can you handle success? Some people can't, and if that's the case, then even the successful business will be a loser. A healthy business has got to grow. Plan now, in your own thinking, just how you will handle or control this growth. Your business is going to grow, whether or not you do in the process. Isn't it better to plan for growth and expansion now while there is no pressure on you and when you have the leisure to do so?

Wouldn't you rather be in control of growth and expansion than have that condition control you? Plan your strategy now, and file it away for your future. Remember, the future is not tomorrow; the future is *now,* and you must begin to ask yourself such questions as: when the business grows, who will assume additional responsibilities? How will you know that they are capable? How will you select leaders? How will you assign leadership roles to others?

13

the small business manager plans for the future

ONE DUTY that cannot be delegated by top management is providing for its own succession as well as the continuity of all human resources within the organization. This responsibility, although often thought to be divorced from the major daily emphasis of management activities, has been recognized by many management theorists as perhaps the most critical duty of management. But in the small firm, management succession is often not given the emphasis it deserves until it is too late. Managers and other key employees cannot be produced overnight.

Where do future managers come from? They can come from outside as well as inside the firm. Sometimes the outsider has a special appeal, especially when the skill needed is new to the organization or is of a very precise technical nature. Of course organizations that routinely fill positions from outside pay a price—the loss of the continued development of those inside the organization. When higher positions are usually filled by outsiders, employees begin to feel that growth opportunities are limited, and they often lose their incentive.

An outsider may appear to be a saint compared with those inside the organization, but he or she also has weaknesses that are more difficult for the organization to spot right off the bat, whereas the weaknesses of the regular employees are well known. Often the new person may come in with fewer political debts and allegiances than someone who is promoted from within, yet it is naive to think that he or she will be free of all political considerations. In addition, the uncertainty of the new person's values often gives rise to additional complications—a feeling-out period. Yet an outsider can provide new ideas and insights.

But if a firm is consistently unable to promote from within, it means that management is falling down in one of its basic duties—planning for succession—either because it does not know how to meet its need or because the planning function is so poor that management is not able to determine what its future human resource needs are. In most organizations there is talent that is capable of assuming additional responsibilities, yet beginning duties in many small firms are characterized by specialized needs and tasks. Indeed, the specialist often commands the highest starting salary because he or she can fill a need immediately. The specialized employee gives the most positive immediate return on investment, yet different jobs require different skills, and the small business manager must always be on the lookout to determine what kinds of human resources will be necessary tomorrow.

Three Categories of Needed Skills[1]

Human skills

No matter what one's level in the organization, the ability to relate to other individuals is crucial. In fact, without some basic

[1] Robert L. Katz, "Skills of an Effective Administrator," *Harvard Business Review*, January–February 1955, pp. 33–42.

human relations skills, one is doomed as a manager. The manager who cannot work with and through other people is like a skilled mechanic who cannot use the proper tools—neither can succeed. Managers cannot accomplish objectives effectively or efficiently without the supportive effort of others. They must have positive relationships with their people if the organization is to be productive for an extended period.

Technical skills

People develop technical skills as they learn to do their jobs, and their expertise grows as they move up the ladder to more responsible positions. Managers need to be proficient in the technical aspects of their jobs, because technical expertise improves their chance for success as leaders. Workers respect a manager who can "do" as well as teach, but they will challenge the word of a leader who doesn't have a firm grasp of the mechanics of the job. Technical proficiency also enables a manager to train other people effectively.

Conceptual skills

This is the skill that is most essential at higher levels of the organization. Someone has to see where the total organization is going, and the higher one gets in an organization, the more important it is to see how the parts fit together to form a workable whole. Conceptual skill is the hardest skill to develop because there is so little opportunity to develop it. In fact, sometimes it may seem as if the organization is doing everything it can to prevent people from seeing the entire picture. Effective management depends on the ability of those assuming management duties to gain appropriate skills.

Most training programs deal with either human skills or specific technical skills. Development of conceptual skills can only come about on the job. One cannot go to school to learn how a company should work. The small business manager should be aware of the need to develop conceptual skills and the important role they can play in the organization. The manager should encourage broader job descriptions and a more flexible organization structure. People should be allowed to poke their noses out of their immediate specialties, and joint departmental and crossfunctional committees should be a matter of course. Emphasis should be on widening people's interest rather than confining them.

Of course, a policy geared to developing conceptual skills can be expensive, and it must be remembered that everyday activities must go on. Therefore, the exposure should be reserved for those who appear to be capable of high achievement. Yet a tricky question remains: "How do I know what potential someone has unless I give him or her a chance to grow?" There is obviously no easy answer to this. Perhaps the best policy is to expose an individual to other duties and functions and then monitor the results.

Providing for the Future

A prerequisite for a future supply of adequate managerial talent is detailed knowledge of just what skills are necessary to perform each of the present job tasks well. In most small organizations the lower the level of the job, the more specific will the analysis of the requirements have to be. As one moves up the organizational hierarchy, jobs become less defined and the job skills required become more nebulous.

Of course, the skills that are really needed to do a job are often unclear, and the requirements may not be pertinent. For this reason it is worthwhile to periodically update the job analysis by actually getting data from those who perform the work, and their picture of the job is matched against the perceptions of management so that differences can be analyzed and revisions made.

If the atmosphere is right and if trust and openness exist, then the next steps should present no difficulty. Once the required key results and the necessary skills of the job are agreed to, employees—in conjunction with their superiors—appraise individual skills in these areas. Deficiencies are noted, and this becomes the basis of a training design.

This form of personnel planning is simple, yet subtle. It involves those most affected by the process in the outcome of the process, and thereby generates employee commitment. Additional care must be taken to make sure that management succession does not take place in a sterile environment, an environment that fails to reflect future realities. Thus, the skills analysis of the job must reflect significant future trends and changes that will affect the firm.

As was noted earlier, the test for higher-level management competency is not easy. The environment of the higher-level job is not as easy to define as that of the lower-level job. A promising technique to spot managerial talent is the assessment center. Here, specific situations calling for responses are posed to the candidate, and the decision pattern is analyzed. Of course, the small firm has its own values, and any standardized analysis must therefore be modified to take account of organizational values. The assessment center offers the promise that perhaps small business managers can develop their own situations and then monitor behavior to see what actions people should take in these situations.

To develop to its fullest potential, good talent needs to be nurtured and assigned additional responsibility and authority. The small business manager owes it to himself, his people, and his business to choose people who are capable of assuming higher duties. It is a slow process with no easy answers, but job rotation, job enlargement, and proper delegation can enhance future human resources.

There is no foolproof way to ensure effective management succession. But if those in positions of authority recognize the importance of career planning and succession, the chances of developing effective strategies can be increased, and potential talent can be spotted and creatively utilized. Management assessment is a promising method to spot talent. By observing management styles and motivation patterns, two key success ingredients can be analyzed. The small business manager would do well to think of those key characteristics that are necessary for successful future performance. Once these values are isolated, he can then develop his own assessment procedures.

14

Far better it is to dare mighty things . . . even though checkered with failure, than to . . . live in the grey twilight that knows not victory nor defeat.

THEODORE ROOSEVELT

the future of small business

SMALL BUSINESS ORGANIZATIONS in the United States face some serious problems in the coming years, and many small business managers have real and justifiable fears about their future prospects. Some of these problems—increased government intervention, the need to train and recruit the right people, the continuing challenge of innovation—will put important choices before small business people. But no matter how many obstacles we face, there are always new opportunities on the horizon.

Increased Government Intervention

Each year interference from all levels of government continues to grow. This is evidenced by the endless parade of regulations that cost much but that provide very little help for the small business person who is making an effort to comply with them. (See the editorial cartoon on the following page for a humorous illustration of this serious point.) Recently many businesses have begun to protest the conflicting orders and directives that are issued by one government agency or another.

The increased cost of completing government paperwork has created many new expenses that are absorbed with no financial return by small businesses. Any time a business is fined for late filing or incomplete reporting, some decision must be made about an appeal: is it worth the time and effort to write to the agency and protest the fine? The answer should be an emphatic "yes." It is worth the time and effort because many penalties are imposed in an arbitrary manner. Computer programs generate notices of fines without regard for individual situations, so the business person who presents a valid case can usually have the penalty abated. There is a feeling of personal pride for the individual business person who is willing to tell government agencies that he or she expects to be treated fairly, not arbitrarily by a computer-generated form letter.

Many statutes in force today apply to all business operations, regardless of size. Interpretation and implementation of these laws, however, can be expensive and time-consuming, and small businesses do not have the kinds of resources that their larger counterparts do. Therefore, the small business person must understand how these laws affect his or her organization, and must avoid the necessity for lengthy legal activities. This can be accomplished by having the responsible agency explain the situation. Agency explanations should be clearly documented so that the business person does indeed understand the business obligation. More small business people should insist on clarification at the agency's expense, rather than at their own expense.

Increasing future government intervention presents one of the major roadblocks to the growth of small business. A satisfactory solution to excess government activity will be found when business people realize that they will be able to make their feelings known through organizational efforts at local, state, and national levels.

One good framework for solving this problem is the various trade and professional organizations. Business people should try to elect representatives who will be sensitive to their needs. Small businesses can become a powerful catalyst for change if each business owner is willing to contribute the time and money necessary to effect change.

The Need to Recruit and Train the Right People

People are the most important asset to any small business, and the future success of management is directly reflected by the caliber of individual employees that the organization can hire. Attracting qualified people is only the starting point. Management's ultimate success will be based in part on innovative training programs that provide *continuing* plans for individual employee career path development within the organization.

Small organizations can provide important ingredients for success rarely found in large companies. In a small company, the right person can take on more responsibility much sooner and an individual's decisions can affect the operation at all levels, not just at or near the top. New employees are visible to top management almost from the time they are hired. Hence, in a small business, *everyone* makes a significant contribution and one that can be easily recognized by upper echelon people. This is not the case in large organizations.

The Continuing Challenge of Innovation

Sometimes people tend to be shortsighted—like the government official who wanted to close the U.S. Patent Office in the late 1800s because he thought that everything had already been invented. A leading manufacturer of computer hardware was also plagued with the same myopic view when in the early 1950s its chief executive estimated the total market for large-scale computers to be somewhere around *thirteen* systems. Fortunately, cooler heads prevailed in these instances, and development continued.

Better ways to do things always exist; the challenge is to find these methods. No one person or group has the market cornered on new ideas. Although many significant new ideas come from large research organizations, the really show-stopping ideas usually begin in the mind of one person. Two examples of this are the Polaroid Land Camera and the Xeroxographic process of copy reproduction. Each of these ideas became an invention which grew very rapidly into a first-rate industry, and volumes have been written about the development of the Polaroid Company and the Xerox Corporation.

Good ideas are difficult to find, but an outstanding idea eventually comes into its own. Many times, these ideas begin as small business operations, which should give some incentive to small business people who are on the lookout for new products and processes.

Opportunity and Small Business Development

When opportunity arises, two principal responses occur. The person with the idea may begin a business with whatever skills are available at that time, and he or she may upgrade skills as the operation grows. Or he or she may go to the marketplace with the idea and hire people who have the necessary skills to make it real.

Like most people, Frank Piasecki used the first approach. When he developed the first successful tandem-rotor helicopter, the work was done in his garage. He went on to found a company that produced hundreds of military and civilian helicopters. Today his organization is a division of the Boeing Company. Frank Piasecki used his own skills and resources up to a point and then used outside resources to start his company. But he was smart enough to take action while the opportunity was there, because opportunity doesn't wait for originators of ideas to become knowledgeable and experienced business people.

Prior Planning and Preparation: A Must in the Future

Today, planning receives more lip service than actual implementation in many small businesses. But in the future, detailed planning and prior preparation will play a vital role in the survival of many companies. In the early days of a new business, the basic operations pattern is established: there is an urgency to "get on with it" and a euphoric feeling that everything will be all right if the business can just get started. But lack of planning lessens the chances for success, and when left to themselves, things go from bad to worse.

Part of the planning process must include a penetrating look at the goals of the business. In-depth planning at this point may well save some small business people from going into business with an unsound idea. Although unpleasant, this early planning process may ensure that those who make the choice are correct in their decision to try and are better equipped to survive in business.

An important part of the American way of life is the chance to provide for ourselves, to do it on our own. The younger generation interprets this concept as "doing your own thing." The chance to go into one's own business certainly provides a way to achieve personal, financial, and career independence, and that is one of its principal benefits.

New Opportunities Are Always on the Horizon

An unlimited range of new business opportunities exists in the future—opportunities that are unknown today. No one can predict the possibilities that result from new ideas. And small business has a key role to play in this process. Big business organizations depend on the small organization for many things, such as new products or new directions for existing products and services. Just as the mighty ship is helpless in certain situations without the aid and guidance of the small tugboat, so it is with the big business: growth in some areas would cease if it were not for the changes and opportunities provided by the small operations.

Preparation: A Key to Future Success

Throughout life, we are reminded to "be prepared." Preparedness cannot be assumed; we must work to maintain our level of readiness in every important area of life. Preparedness is synonymous with survival for the future small business manager. People in small business need to maintain their level of readiness in every important area of business. They must also be ready to upgrade their skills level on a continuing basis, as conditions change. One aspect of preparedness involves a high degree of expertise in dealing with employees. This could well mean a program of continuing education where new theories are acquired in the classroom environment.

The future of small business is full of challenging opportunities. Despite many drawbacks (including excessive government regulation, saturation competition, rising costs in all areas, and a lack of developmental capital), there are more small business operations today than ever before. People like to be treated as individuals, and they object to being "just a number" in their places of business. Large organizations either cannot or will not provide individual treatment, but the small business can provide personal service to its customers. This is the basis for its success: it shows each customer just how important he or she is. And in a world of massive bureaucracies and growing depersonalization, that quality is very precious indeed.

Appendix

your "build a winning team" management workbook

THE EXERCISES in this workbook should help you put into practice many of the most important concepts discussed in this book. They correspond to some of the basic ideas and should be done in conjunction with the chapter in the text in which those concepts appear. (References appear in the text itself.) Some of these topics include change and its effect on you, how your actions affect employee self-esteem, the value of management education, the ability to motivate people, delegating responsibility, managing your time, and determining your own motivational pattern.

Forces for Change—Internal and External

List the *internal* factors that you think will influence change in your organization in the near future.

1. _____

2. _____

3. _____

4. _____

5. _____

List the *external* factors that you think will influence change in your organization in the foreseeable future. (Compare your list with the one immediately following, and revise if necessary.)

1. _____

2. _____

3. _____

4. _____

5. _____

Larger External Trends That Will Influence Change in Organizations

1. A greatly increased standard of living in the United States and throughout the world.
2. An increasing gap between the powerful and rich, and the powerless and poor.
3. A rapid increase in the world population.
4. Continued changes in value systems.
5. The greater expectation of people for services in general, but for health care in particular.
6. The increased influence of local, state, and federal governments.
7. An increased desire for power by minority groups.
8. A continued increase in the influence of mass media.
9. The extensive development of education as it applies to continued growth and development at all ages.
10. A shift from a production to a service economy.
11. A continued increase in technology.
12. An increased activism by consumers.
13. The development of new vocations and avocations in society.
14. An increased interdependence of all nations.
15. A continuation of ecological concerns.
16. An increased mobility of people and a lessening of commitment to any one organization or community.
17. An increased size of social systems so that people will feel more and more powerless.
18. A continued explosion of knowledge.
19. The desire for quality, not just quantity, as a goal in life.
20. Limitations on energy usage.

Adapted from Gordon L. Lippitt, "Hospital Organization in the Post-Industrial Society," *Hospital Progress*, June 1973.

How These Changes Will Affect You

Take your list of anticipated internal and external changes, examine it, and for each change you have listed, ask yourself the following series of questions. This is a good way of determining how these changes will really affect all aspects of your life, and it will help train you to anticipate change and to plan for the future systematically.

1. How will my advancement possibilities change?
2. How will my salary change?
3. How will my future with this company change?
4. How will my view of myself change?
5. How will my formal authority change?
6. How will my informal influence change?

7. How will my view of my prior values change?
8. How will my ability to predict the future change?
9. How will my status change?
10. How will what my family thinks of me change?
11. How will the amount of work I do change?
12. How will my interest in the work change?

13. How will the importance of my work change?
14. How will the challenge of the work change?
15. How will the work pressures change?
16. How will the skill demands on me change?
17. How will my physical surroundings change?
18. How will my hours of work change?

Adapted from W. J. Redin, *Managerial Effectiveness.* New York: McGraw-Hill, 1970. p. 163.

Which Managerial Type Are You? The Three-Role Approach

A good way to determine what kind of a manager you are is the three-role approach. The following chart shows characteristic emotions, goals, standards of evaluation, and techniques of influence of three basic types of manager. Try to determine which of them describes you best.

	Tough Battler	*Friendly Helper*	*Objective Thinker*
Emotions	Accepts aggression, rejects affection	Accepts affection, rejects aggression	Rejects both affection and aggression
Goal	Dominance	Acceptance	Correctness
Operates by	Direction, intimidation, control of rewards	Offering understanding, praise, favors, friendship	Factual data; logical arguments
Value in organization	Initiates, demands, disciplines	Supports, harmonizes, relieves tension	Defines, clarifies, gets information, criticizes, tests
Overuses	Fight	Kindness	Analysis
Becomes	Pugnacious	Sloppy, sentimental	Pedantic
Fears	Being soft or dependent	Desertion, conflict	Emotions, irrational acts
Needs	Warmth, consideration, objectivity, humility	Strength, integrity, firmness, self-assertion	Awareness of ability to love and fight

Each managerial type has its own advantages and disadvantages, and each is susceptible to exaggeration and distortion. For instance, the Tough Battler would be a better manager, a better parent, a better neighbor, and a more satisfied person if he or she could learn some sensitivity, accept inevitable dependence on others, and have some consideration for other people. Such a manager would be more successful by recognizing that some situations will not yield to pugnacity alone.

On the other hand, Friendly Helpers would be better managers, parents, citizens, and people if they could stand up for their own interests and for what was right, even against the pleas of others. What they need is firmness and strength and the courage not to evade or to smooth over conflicts. They must learn to face the facts. Objective Thinkers would be better people if they could become more aware of their own feelings and of the feelings of others around them. They need to learn that there are times when it is all right to fight and other times when it is desirable to love. This chart should help you evaluate your strengths and weaknesses and allow you to pinpoint where you need to change.

Management Attitude Questionnaire

The following twelve questions give a basic view of the small business manager's assumptions about people.

	Strongly Disagree	*Disagree*	*Agree*	*Strongly Agree*
1. It's only human nature for people to try to do as little as they can get away with.	1 ( )	2 ( )	3 ( )	4 ( )
2. It's too much to expect that people will try to do a good job without being prodded by their boss.	1 ( )	2 ( )	3 ( )	4 ( )
3. One problem in asking for the ideas of subordinates is that their perspective is too limited for their suggestions to be of much practical value.	1 ( )	2 ( )	3 ( )	4 ( )
4. Because most people don't like to make decisions on their own, it's hard to get them to assume responsibility	1 ( )	2 ( )	3 ( )	4 ( )
5. If people don't use much imagination and ingenuity on the job, it's probably because relatively few people have much of either.	1 ( )	2 ( )	3 ( )	4 ( )
6. Being tough with people will usually get them to do what you want.	1 ( )	2 ( )	3 ( )	4 ( )
7. A good way to get people to do more work is to crack down on them once in a while.	1 ( )	2 ( )	3 ( )	4 ( )

	Strongly Disagree	Disagree	Agree	Strongly Agree
8. The most effective supervisor is one who gets the results management expects, regardless of the methods he uses in handling people.	1 ( )	2 ( )	3 ( )	4 ( )
9. It weakens a man's prestige when he has to admit that a subordinate has been right and he has been wrong.	1 ( )	2 ( )	3 ( )	4 ( )
10. Even when given encouragement by the boss, very few people show the desire to improve themselves on the job.	1 ( )	2 ( )	3 ( )	4 ( )
11. If you give people enough money, they are less likely to worry about such intangibles as status or individual recognition.	1 ( )	2 ( )	3 ( )	4 ( )
12. The boss who expects his people to set their own standards for superior performance will probably find they set them pretty low.	1 ( )	2 ( )	3 ( )	4 ( )

Total your point score—it can range from 12 to 48. The lower your score, the more pronounced your Y orientation. The higher your score, the higher your X orientation. (For the basic components of each of these outlooks, see Chapter 6.)

Self-Assessment Guide:
Do You Help Build or Wreck Employee Confidence?

The small business manager needs to build esteem and confidence in employees—for his own sake and for the sake of the company. But it's easy to fall into problems in this area, and many managers unconsciously tear down employees when they should be encouraging them. The first guide lists several ways that managers tear employees down; the second contrasts a negative approach with a positive one.

Twelve Ways to Wreck Employee Confidence

1. Tell your subordinates what you want in terms so vague that they cannot pinpoint precisely what you want.

2. Give an audible sigh of resignation or act shocked if they ask you to clarify some point.

3. If they ask the same question more than once, point out that you have already answered it.

4. Make an obvious effort to contain your impatience if they do not understand.

5. Criticize petty specific errors.

6. Do not explain the purpose or the expected result of their jobs.

7. Change instructions often.

8. Assign them jobs below their ability and training.

9. Assign them jobs above their ability and training.

10. Give them unrealistic deadlines.

11. Improve on everything they do.

12. Make them do each job your way.

Do's and Don'ts in Building Up Employee Self-Esteem

Don'ts	*Do's*

Treating an Employee as an Individual

Don'ts	*Do's*
Ignore the employee: fail to speak to employee; ignore suggestions; keep employee waiting	Notice employee: notice, even though busy; encourage suggestions; keep appointments promptly
Treat impersonally	Call employee by name
Show no interest	Draw out in conversation
Break promises	Keep all promises

Giving Deserved Recognition

Don'ts	*Do's*
Fail to give credit when due	Be prompt in giving credit
Praise results only	Recognize effort as well as achievement
Blame unfairly	Be cautious in placing the blame
Fail to see potentialities	Encourage initiative and talent
Fail to let employee know progress	Let employee know how he is doing

Avoiding Behavior That Demeans People

Don'ts	*Do's*
Assume a bossy attitude: speak in a loud voice; use fear as a weapon; dictate	Treat employee as co-worker: talk *with*, not *at*, employee; suggest; speak in moderate tones; avoid use of threats
Appear too busy to listen	Take time to listen attentively
Criticize thoughtlessly: criticize in public; criticize personally; criticize only negatively	Criticize tactfully: criticize in private; be objective and impersonal; criticize constructively; allow employee to correct own mistakes; give criticism when needed
Anticipate failure	Make employee feel he will succeed
Use sarcasm or ridicule	Avoid playing up oneself at employee's expense

Are You an Effective Motivator?

To determine how effective you are as a motivator, answer the following questions by putting an "X" in the proper column. Do not look at the next series of questions until you have finished answering these.

	Yes	No
1. Do you honestly feel that most of your people don't want to work?		
2. Do they perform their jobs inefficiently?		
3. Do they often make mistakes even when instructed?		
4. Are they often hard to handle?		
5. Do they frequently seem to be disorganized?		
6. Do they stand around while you do all the work?		
7. Do they often misunderstand your motives?		
8. Do you find that your people are often disloyal?		
9. Does morale seem generally poor among your people?		

This next quiz is closely related to the first one. Examine your answers to the first quiz, and in each case fill in the *opposite* response on the second one. (For example, if you answered "Yes" to question 1 on the first quiz, you should answer "no" to question 1 on the second quiz, and so on.)

	Yes	No
1. Are you able to motivate your people?		
2. Have you trained them effectively?		
3. Do you issue orders and instruct clearly?		
4. Are you maintaining effective control?		
5. Are you a capable work and manpower organizer?		
6. Do you delegate work and responsibility properly?		
7. Are you communicating properly with your people?		
8. Have you won the confidence of your people?		
9. Have you developed spirit and team play among your people?		

How to Make Management Education Pay Off

Is your organization getting all the benefits it can from attendance at management training and development programs? Or is some of your investment going down the drain because line management and the personnel or training function are not doing what they should? With a well-planned and executed company development policy and management development procedure, you can reap rich rewards from the time and money you spend on management education. To ensure maximum return on your investment in management education, here are a few simple procedures to follow.

1. *Review potential benefits.* For the organization, this should result in better management, higher productivity, improved profitability, better employee morale, and improved company image (a valuable asset in attracting the best candidates for positions at all levels). For the individual, it should mean increased knowledge of the best management philosophies and principles, improved management skills, better management attitude, and improved performance. Tangible rewards should include salary increases, promotions, personal growth, and greater job satisfaction.

2. *Review available programs.* Find out what programs are available and learn as much as possible about the sponsoring organizations. Review and evaluate the programs and how they relate to your organizational and individual needs. Check promotional materials for program content. Determine the quality of the speakers and conference leaders. Invest your training dollars in programs of proven benefit.

3. *Select participants.* Carefully select those who will attend the programs, only sending people who are likely to benefit most by attending. Match individual desires and needs with program content and objectives. If your firm is large enough, seek staff advice: ask your personnel manager, training director, and other qualified staff persons to help judge the availability and quality of programs. Have line managers and staff people jointly determine who should attend and get maximum benefit.

4. *Plan ahead.* It's a good idea to plan your participation six months or a year ahead of time, so that you can do a better job of matching needs to available programs and you can budget accurately for fees and expenses. Finally, you can make sure that space will be available in the programs that you want to attend. (Many of the most beneficial programs reach the maximum enrollment several weeks before the program is held.)

5. *Meet with the participant before the program.* It is very important to have open communication between participants and their immediate supervisors. This should begin with precounseling, perhaps with a personnel or training person as a third party. Precounseling serves several purposes: it indicates your interest and confidence in the employee's development, and it gives you an opportunity to communicate what each of you expect as a result of the program. During the interview, discuss program details—when and where the program will be held and how to get maximum benefits. Participants should give both a written report (evaluating the program and content as well as possible applications) and an oral report (to a boss or a group), and should discuss new ideas or procedures.

6. *Discuss the program with the participant afterwards.* After the program, be sure the immediate supervisor takes time to discuss the program with the participant to get his reaction, a summary of the program's content, and possible ideas to implement. Also, the supervisor should take an interest in handout material that can serve as follow-up reading. Supervisors should offer to help implement the ideas. Nothing is as frustrating to a participant returning from a program as a supervisor who shows little or no interest in the program that a subordinate has just attended.

7. *Help the participant plan for future development.* Finally, help the participant plan an ongoing personal development program. This can include reading and special job assignments, as well as attendance at future relevant programs.

Adapted from Donald Kirkpatrick, *Obtaining Maximum Benefits from Outside Management Development Programs.* Milwaukee: University of Wisconsin, Milwaukee Extension, 1976.

Delegating Responsibility

The next series of quizzes concerns the all-important question of delegating responsibility, a very basic problem for small business managers. Answer these questions as honestly as possible—even if the answers aren't flattering. For in order to make improvements, we must first discover our weaknesses.

Check Your Skill in Delegating Responsibility

	Yes	No
1. I have trained employees to plan ahead, and sudden, unexpected emergencies are rare in my opinion.	____	____
2. Simple jobs that are part of the regular routine are delegated and promptly done. Little follow-up is required.	____	____
3. Details are not my headache. I have employees who are capable of handling them.	____	____
4. There is little friction or discontent in my work team. We work together smoothly and cooperatively.	____	____
5. My advance planning relieves the pressure of the daily job and gives me time to think out future assignments.	____	____
6. I never pass the buck for my own mistakes but accept full responsibility when operations fail to go as I have planned.	____	____
7. When I am not present, my group continues to function efficiently. Work doesn't come to a stop until I return.	____	____
8. My employees are self-starters. On familiar jobs, they don't wait for orders to go ahead. However, if an assignment is new or complicated, they are careful to be checked out properly before they start work.	____	____
9. Employees frequently give me good suggestions for operational improvements.	____	____
10. My group has high morale, spontaneity in their work habits and an attitude of good humor, mutual liking and respect in their associations with each other and with me.	____	____

The more "yes" answers you gave, the better a delegator you are.

Are You an Effective Delegator?

		Yes	*No*
1.	I tell my subordinates what I want in terms so vague that they cannot pinpoint precisely what I want.	____	____
2.	I give an audible sigh of resignation or act shocked if a subordinate asks me to clarify some point.	____	____
3.	If a subordinate asks the same question more than once, I point out that I have already answered it.	____	____
4.	I make an obvious effort to contain my impatience if he does not understand.	____	____
5.	I criticize petty, specific errors made by subordinates.	____	____
6.	I do not explain the purpose or the expected result of the job to subordinates.	____	____
7.	I change instructions often to subordinates.	____	____
8.	I assign subordinates jobs below their ability and training.	____	____
9.	I assign subordinates jobs above their ability and training.	____	____
10.	I give subordinates unrealistic deadlines.	____	____
11.	I improve on everything subordinates do.	____	____
12.	I make subordinates do each job my way.	____	____
13.	Have I skipped any vacations in the last five years?	____	____
14.	Do I work longer hours than those reporting to me?	____	____
15.	Do I usually work at home?	____	____
16.	Am I usually behind in my work?	____	____
17.	Do I measure success primarily by time worked rather than accomplishments?	____	____
18.	Do my people request advice once or twice a day?	____	____
19.	Do their questions to me involve details rather than policies?	____	____
20.	Do my people hesitate to make recommendations to me?	____	____
21.	Are job descriptions for my people of the activity type?	____	____
22.	Do my people accomplish less than 75% of their objectives?	____	____
23.	Do I overrule my people regularly?	____	____

	Yes	No
24. Do I check on their work frequently?	___	___
25. Do I hold frequent staff meetings?	___	___
26. Do I evaluate on "personality"?	___	___
27. Is my department plagued by slow decision making?	___	___
28. Are needed decisions postponed when I am away?	___	___
29. Do I permit my people to select their own means to agreed-upon ends?	___	___
30. Do I grant my people the right to be wrong?	___	___
31. Do my people know specifically the results they must achieve?	___	___
32. Are they consistently qualified for the promotions they get?	___	___
33. Has their authority been clearly defined?	___	___
34. Is it in writing?	___	___
35. Did my people recommend it to me?	___	___
36. Do I reward based on results?	___	___
37. Do my subordinates have effective responsibility accounting?	___	___
38. Do they have a major voice in determining their roles?	___	___
39. Is people development a major concern as I delegate?	___	___
40. Do I really know the strengths and weaknesses of my people?	___	___
41. Do I base my judgments on this?	___	___
42. Do I consult with them prior to setting my own objectives?	___	___
43. Would I be willing to let my subordinates answer the same questions for me?	___	___
44. If I were a subordinate, would I be happy working for myself?	___	___

If you answered "no" to questions 1 through 28, and "yes" to questions 29 through 44, you're a good delegator and should have a smooth-running operation. If you feel your delegation needs to be improved, however, you can now start practicing the good management traits suggested by these questions.

Adapted from University of Wisconsin, Milwaukee Extension, Continuing Education Program Schedule, Fall 1976.

Managing Your Time Effectively:
A List of Suggestions

1. Write daily "to-do" list—including top priorities.

2. On Mondays, plan a whole week's work.

3. Have your secretary screen your mail and phone calls.

4. Delegate routine chores.

5. Set deadlines for subordinates when you delegate projects to them.

6. Set deadlines for yourself.

7. Use waiting time to plan projects for the rest of the day.

8. Carry blank 3 x 5 cards to jot down spontaneous notes and ideas.

9. When you procrastinate, ask yourself what you're avoiding. Break unpleasant tasks into small nonthreatening jobs.

10. Cut off nonproductive activities such as phone calls, rambling conversations.

11. Put up reminder signs to keep yourself on task. Example: Are You Daydreaming? Keep Phone Calls Brief!

12. Handle every piece of paper only once. Immediately throw away what you don't need; don't mull over it.

13. Answer mail by writing comments on each letter. Have your secretary complete the correspondence.

14. Keep your desk cleared and ready for action. Items waiting for attention should be in the middle of the desk.

15. Have a place for everything so you know immediately where to find it.

16. Schedule meetings only when they inform, solve a problem, or sell an idea. Replace other meetings with memos.

17. When you read, skim for important words, headlines.

18. Listen carefully. Ask direct questions to obtain needed information quickly.

19. Learn to say no to colleagues if they ask for help on projects and you're already involved in too many things.

20. Do your thinking on paper. It helps to organize and motivates you to continue because you can see progress.

21. Set aside your most productive time period each day for creative work.

22. Ask help from specialists (engineers, accountants, marketing executives, etc.) when working on special problems.

23. Write letters to people who regularly talk too long on the phone.

24. Move your desk so it faces away from your office door. This discourages you from looking every time someone passes and others from stopping in your doorway to chat.

25. Make it clear that unannounced "drop-ins" aren't welcome.

26. Try to arrive at your office a half hour early each day to take advantage of the quiet time before other employees arrive.

Source: University of Wisconsin, Milwaukee Extension, Continuing Education Program Schedule, Fall 1976.

index